BALLETS RUSSES

BALLETS RUSSES

GREENWICH EDITIONS

A QUANTUM BOOK

Published by Greenwich Editions
10 Blenheim Court
Brewery Road
London N7 9NT

Copyright ©1989 Quarto Publishing plc

This edition printed 1998

All rights reserved.

This book is protected by copyright. No part of it
may be reproduced, stored in a retrieval system, or
transmitted in any form or by any means, without the
prior permission in writing of the Publisher, nor be
otherwise circulated in any form of binding or cover
other than that in which it is published and without a
similar condition including this condition being
imposed on the subsequent publisher.

ISBN 0-86288-108-0

QUMBAL

This book is produced by
Quantum Books Ltd
6 Blundell Street
London N7 9BH

Creative Director: Peter Bridgewater
Art Director: Ian Hunt
Designer: Stuart Walden
Editorial Director: Jeremy Harwood
Senior Editor: Sally MacEachern
Editor: Christine Shuttleworth
Picture Manager: Joanna Wiese
Picture Researcher: Deirdre O'Day

Typeset by
Central Southern Typesetters, Eastbourne
Manufactured in Hong Kong by
Regent Publishing Services Ltd
Printed in China by Leefung-Asco Printers Ltd

Contents

FOREWORD	7
THE BIRTH OF A TRADITION	8
TRIUMPH IN THE WEST	18
THE STRUGGLE TO SURVIVE	72
CLASSICISM, NEOCLASSICISM AND EXPERIMENT	108
AFTER DIAGHILEV	176
INDEX AND ACKNOWLEDGMENTS	188

Foreword

'I am, firstly, a charlatan, though rather a brilliant one; secondly, a great charmer; thirdly, frightened of nobody; fourthly, a man with plenty of logic and very few scruples; fifthly, I seem to have no real talent. None the less, I believe that I have found my true vocation – to be a Maecenas. I have everything necessary except money – but that will come!'
Sergei Pavlovitch Diaghilev to his stepmother, Elena Panaev-Diaghilev, in 1895.

THIS IS A BOOK about the *Ballets Russes*, not a biography of Diaghilev. That task has been attempted many times already, and it would be a fool who tried to compete with Richard Buckle's authoritative, detailed and brilliant study. However, without the qualities Diaghilev ironically ascribed to himself in a letter to his stepmother – which can be translated as drive, determination, charm, resourcefulness, taste and ruthlessness – it is highly doubtful that the *Ballets Russes* as Western Europe and the Americas came to know them would ever have existed at all. Many men and women of talent and, in some cases, genius made their contributions to the emergence of this unique artistic phenomenon, but it was Diaghilev's iron will that saw the project through. It follows from this that, without him, the New York City Ballet, the Royal Ballet, the Paris Opéra Ballet and other distinguished companies would not exist, at least in their present form. Nor was the influence of his company confined to the world of ballet alone. This is why any account of the Russian Ballet outside Russia must start with him, though, happily, it did not end with his death.

Sergei Pavlovitch Diaghilev, c1924

CHAPTER ONE

The Birth of a Tradition

ABOVE: *Interior of the Maryinsky Theatre, St Petersburg*

RIGHT: *Pencil drawing of Leon Bakst waiting for a train in St Petersburg, by Alexandre Benois*

THE RUSSIAN LOVE for dancing and gift for it are well attested. It is a received idea, but true. Much nonsense has been written about the innate rhythmic vitality of certain peoples and races, but one has only to compare a Ukrainian *gopak* with, say, Morris-dancing, or a Bavarian *Schuhplattler*, to make the point. In music too, the mainspring of dance, the principle applies. Despite all its magnificence, the German musical school has never been notable for purely rhythmic interest. Even when German music goes all out for rhythmic excitement, one is usually aware behind it of the rather lumbering, not to say lumpish, metres of the *Volkslied*, the military march, the jolly tavern drinking-song. Compare, for instance, the *Carmina Burana* with *The Rite of Spring* or, better still, *Les Noces*, which Orff's work so shamelessly pillages. It could be argued that the two Stravinsky works are extreme cases, as indeed they are; but they are only extreme examples of a tendency to be found consistently in Russian music from Glinka onwards. This music derives its vitality from the folk tradition that nourishes it. The immensely violent *Adoration de la Terre* section of the *Rite* has its roots in an astonishing passage at the end of the Caucasian *Lezginka* in *Ruslan and Ludmila*, written well over half a century before. Speaking of *Lezginkas*, even Khachaturian's crude *Gayane* has rhythmic vitality, if not much else.

THE INFLUENCE OF THE WEST

Though the Russian gift for dance made Russian men and women wonderful raw material for ballet, ballet was in no sense a Russian invention. When, thanks to the dynamism of Peter the Great, Russia was opened up in the 18th century to Western European artistic and literary ideas, it was French and Italian dancers and teachers who came to Russia and set up their schools.

Jean-Baptiste Landé came to St Petersburg in 1734 to teach ballroom dancing, and four years later opened a ballet school for the children of palace servants: this eventually became the Imperial Ballet School and the company of the Maryinsky (now the Kirov) Theatre. Similarly, in 1773, a dance wing was attached to the Orphanage at Moscow. This was the origin of the Bolshoi School and Ballet. In addition, many wealthy landowners had private theatres in their houses with troupes of dancers made up of 'attractive and well-formed people from among the house servants or orphans'. The interest of the landowners in the charms of their good-looking serfs was not necessarily purely aesthetic: 'Prince Nicholas Yusupov liked to amuse his friends with his serf ballet. After the performance on the stage he would give a signal and the entire *corps de ballet* would appear before the spectators in their natural state. This brought forth great delight, and an orgy followed.' The serf theatres, which were very

The Birth of a Tradition

numerous (20 in Moscow alone towards the end of the 18th century) were fine sources of material for the Imperial Theatres, and landowners often sold or gave their best dancers to the government. Before the liberation of the serfs in 1861, most of the outstanding dancers had been bought by the Imperial Theatres, and the private dance troupes gradually became a thing of the past.

In 1801 the Frenchman Charles-Louis Didelot, who had studied under Vestris and Noverre, came to St Petersburg and spent 10 years reorganizing the whole system of ballet teaching and laying the foundations of the St Petersburg school style. He spent a further 17 years there from 1816 to 1833 – a period that marked the first great epoch of ballet in the city. The phenomenon of balletomania made its first appearance in history, the balletomanes including, not only the officers of the St Petersburg Guards regiments, but also many distinguished civilians, including the poet Alexander Pushkin. He seldom missed a ballet performance, and was proud that his poem *The Prisoner of the Caucasus* was the basis of a ballet by Didelot in 1823. By now ballet in Russia had attained an importance and a social and artistic standing which it retained throughout the 19th century (and which it has never lost), even when the art went into a serious decline in France, Italy and England. It was this vigorous Russian strain which was eventually to breathe life back into the ballet in its original Western homes.

PETIPA: LINK BETWEEN OLD AND NEW

The Western influence continued with the arrival of Taglioni in St Petersburg to make her debut in *La Sylphide* in 1837. After her farewell performance in 1842 one of her admirers bought a pair of her ballet shoes and had them cooked, served with a special sauce, and offered them to his friends at a balletomanes' supper. Tsar Nicholas I sent her a cape of Yakoutsk sables. Perrot and Saint-Léon worked at St Petersburg, but the most important event of all in the history of Russian 19th-century ballet was the arrival of Marius Petipa. Born in Marseilles, he came from a family of dancers, and was already famous as a performer, choreographer and ballet master when he came to Russia in 1847. He remained there until his death in 1910. He was a direct link between Vestris and Diaghilev: he had been a pupil of the former, and the latter presented his greatest ballet, *The Sleeping Beauty*, to a Western audience for the first time in 1921. For some 40 years, from the 1860s on, Petipa dominated the Imperial Ballet School and the Imperial Theatres, which, in essence, belonged to the Tsar.

In pre-revolutionary Russia the key theatres for ballet were the Maryinsky and the Bolshoi. They were controlled, as were the theatres presenting Russian, French and German drama and Italian opera, by the Chancellery of His Majesty; this formed part of the responsibility of the Minister of the Imperial Court, who answered directly to the Tsar. The fact that the Director of the Imperial Theatres ran them primarily for the pleasure of the Imperial Family and their courts (of which there were 19 at the beginning of the 20th century) gave them prestige and respectability; the other, and inevitable, side of the coin was a tendency towards bureaucracy and ossification. But ballet remained an important part of Russian artistic life, dignified by the Tsar's patronage. Meanwhile in Western Europe ballet went into decline. The last important ballets created in Paris in the 19th century were those of Delibes: *Coppélia* (1870) and *Sylvia* (1876). Already male roles were being given to women dancing *en travestie*: Franz in *Coppélia* was an example. There were ballets, of a sort, in many operas, but ballet had little or no independent artistic life and turned primarily into an insipid entertainment designed to enable rich old men to ogle their favourite young dancers. In England ballet was regarded as an adjunct to the music-hall. In Italy – at Milan, in particular – the situation was technically somewhat better. But only in Russia and in one other country did ballet retain its dignity. The other country was Denmark, but since the wonders of the Bournonville repertoire were practically unknown to the outside world until the mass visit of British ballet critics in 1951 and the subsequent Danish season at Covent Garden in 1953, what was going on in Denmark had no influence anywhere else.

A choreographer of genius, as is now recognized, Petipa was a despot and became – as was natural – progressively more conservative. His composers – of whom perhaps Pugni and Minkus were the best, which speaks for itself – wrote directly to the choreographer's detailed specifications, and the result was predictably undistinguished, though a composer of genius, Tchaikovsky, proved later that, given sufficient inspiration, one could overcome and even derive benefit from such direct instructions. Scenery and costumes were the work of professional scene-painters, not artists in any real sense of the word. Male dancing as a feature of the ballets was very much neglected, but – and this is extremely important – roles were not danced *en travestie* and male dancers continued to be trained as thoroughly as women.

Outside factors gradually had an effect on Petipa's ideas. In the 1880s and 1890s several very brilliant Italian dancers appeared at St Petersburg: these included Virginia Zucchi, Pierina Legnani, Carlotta

Portrait of Alexandre Benois by Leon Bakst

Brianza and Enrico Cecchetti, whose exceptional technique reminded the St Petersburg audience of the feats of which male dancers were capable. He became second ballet master of the Imperial Theatres in 1890, began to teach in 1892, and created the roles of the Blue Bird and Carabosse in *The Sleeping Beauty*. Cecchetti was to have many brilliant pupils, including Nijinsky, Pavlova and Karsavina, and eventually became Diaghilev's *maître de ballet*. Petipa absorbed the almost 'acrobatic' innovations of the newcomers into his style.

Another event, and one of extreme importance, was the appearance of Tchaikovsky as a ballet composer in St Petersburg. *Le Lac des Cygnes* had been presented at the Bolshoi Theatre in Moscow in 1877, but achieved no great success. But *The Sleeping Beauty*, first performed on 15 and 16 January, 1890 (the first date was that of the public dress rehearsal), revealed to the Maryinsky audience the genius of the greatest composer of ballet music of all time (Stravinsky is his only possible rival), and aroused the enthusiasm of a whole group of artistically talented young people who had hitherto regarded the Imperial Ballet as hopelessly rigid and divorced from life, frozen in an unreal, outdated world of its own.

Tamara Karsavina, 1914

THE YOUNG DIAGHILEV

Among these young people was Léon Bakst, who secured an invitation to the dress rehearsal thanks to his friendship with the elderly chief stage-manager. The shy young student was introduced to Tchaikovsky and the performance made a profound impression on him. 'That evening, I believe', he wrote 30 years later, 'my vocation was determined.' Tchaikovsky's masterpiece thus played a crucial role in the career of the man who was to become the greatest stage designer of the 20th century. Alexandre Benois went to the second or third performance with his friend Vladimir (Dima) Filosofov. Deeply impressed by the ballet, Benois returned again and again. It is highly likely that among the audience at one of these performances was Dima's rather provincial cousin, newly arrived from the country, Sergei Pavlovitch Diaghilev.

Between them, Bakst and Benois were to design the most famous and spectacular sets and costumes for Diaghilev's first ballet seasons in the West. Another of the group, Walter Nuvel, became an invaluable administrative and financial aide to Diaghilev. But all this was very much in the future, and the young men were inclined to look down a little on the newcomer, albeit in an affectionate way. In his *Memoirs* Benois writes:

'There was not the faintest likeness between the slight, pale Dima and his cousin, who impressed us rather by his fresh and healthy appearance. He had red cheeks and dazzling white teeth which formed two even rows between his scarlet lips. When he laughed the whole "inside" of his jaws seemed to be flung wide open. Serioja laughed like a child, often, and on any pretext. He was obviously highly excited at finding himself in the capital and at meeting the closest friends of a cousin with whom he had corresponded assiduously for some years . . . He seemed to us a "good fellow", a lusty provincial, perhaps not very intelligent, rather primitive, but on the whole quite likeable.'

But Benois and the others soon became aware that Diaghilev had an extraordinary capacity for absorbing the ideas of others and making them his own. They also realized that he was, above all, a fighter. For the moment, however, they saw little of him, for he set off with his cousin Dima, with whom he was in love, on a European tour which took them to the cities of Berlin, Paris, Venice, Rome, Florence and Vienna.

Diaghilev was born on 17 March, 1872, in the Selistchev Barracks in the Province of Novgorod. His father was a professional soldier who rose to the rank of lieutenant-general and became an ADC to the Tsar. He was also very musical and, for instance, knew *Ruslan and Ludmila* by heart. Diaghilev's mother died a few days after his birth, and his father married again two years later, but the little boy's stepmother was kindly and sympathetic. He grew to manhood at Perm, 1,000 miles from St Petersburg, with only the Urals between the town and Siberia: a provincial capital where his father commanded the garrison. The Diaghilev family was noble, technically speaking, but in no way of any great importance.

On his return from Europe to St Petersburg, Diaghilev enrolled at the University and started to study law, which interested him hardly at all; he also began singing lessons with a baritone called Cotogni and studied composition with Rimsky-Korsakov. In the end he abandoned both, Rimsky-Korsakov having told him, kindly but unambiguously, that he had no talent for writing music. But the knowledge of music he had gained was invaluable to him in the future.

It was becoming clear that Diaghilev's future was going to lie in the world of the arts, but there was no indication at this stage that it was the ballet that was going to preoccupy him. It comes as a shock to those of us who will always associate his name with the dance, and who regard his career, with all its setbacks, disappointments and even tragedies, as essentially a triumph, to find Benois writing as follows in 1930, the year after Diaghilev's death:

'For me he wasn't Diaghilev, he was Serge, Serioja, a "boy" who developed as I watched into a superb man of

Vaslav Nijinsky as a young man

action, who would certainly have accomplished a much more important and much more glorious mission if the incoherence of Russian life before the Revolution and the tragic events which came afterwards had not made him a stranger in his own country and turned him into a "manager" specializing in choreography, obliged to take the works created under his direction around the world.'

It is salutary to read this statement, though one has to bear in mind that Benois was out of sympathy with the aesthetic of the later Diaghilev ballets.

Diaghilev's first entrepreneurial activity was to arrange, in January 1897, an exhibition of German and British watercolours at the Stieglitz Museum. This was followed by a further exhibition, of Russian and Finnish paintings, at the Museum in early 1898. That same year, Diaghilev obtained enough financial backing to make arrangements to publish a magazine which was called *Mir Iskusstva* (*The World of Art*). The first number appeared in November and the magazine continued until 1904. It was of great importance in Russian artistic history and was to fulfil the double function of revealing Russian art to the Russians themselves and showing them new artistic developments in the West. While getting *Mir Iskusstva* off the ground Diaghilev some- how found time to organize yet a third show at the Stieglitz Museum, this time an International Exhibition of Russian, Finnish, Swedish, Norwegian, German, Belgian, American, Italian, British and French paintings. This opened in January 1899.

By now Diaghilev had been presented to the Tsar and other members of the Imperial Family, and in 1899 Prince Sergei Mikhailovitch Volkonsky, the newly appointed Director of the Imperial Theatres, took Diaghilev on to his staff as a 'functionary for special missions'. This appointment appears to have gone somewhat to Diaghilev's head, and it was short-lived. His first task was to edit the next edition of the *Theatres Annual*, a dull affair which provided a record of the year's performances at the subsidized theatres in St Petersburg and Moscow. Diaghilev turned it into a *de luxe* publication which created a sensation, even though in so doing he exceeded his budget by 50 per cent.

But Diaghilev was beginning to make enemies. He prevailed on Volkonsky to give him control of a new production of Delibes' ballet *Sylvia*, which he and his friends admired. Benois and Bakst were to work on the production. But Volkonsky was faced with so much internal opposition that he felt obliged to retract his promise. Diaghilev took violent offence and embarked on a series of intrigues, which resulted in his summary dismissal under a clause normally used only to punish serious improprieties.

One of the people Diaghilev involved in his plottings was Matilda Kchessinskaya, the *prima ballerina assoluta* of the Maryinsky. She had been the mistress of Nicholas II before he had ascended the throne, and was now being kept by the Grand Duke Andrei Vladimirovitch. She was also on excellent terms with the Grand Dukes Sergei Mikhailovitch and Vladimir Alexandrovitch, and was thus in a perfect position to make life agreeable or disagreeable, depending on her whim, for anyone whose career brought him within the orbit of the Imperial Theatres. She did not hesitate to do the latter where Diaghilev was concerned, a little later, but at the time she was disposed to like him. In her somewhat disingenuous memoirs (*Dancing in St Petersburg*) she speaks of her affection for him and the fact that when 'Chinchilla' (as he was nicknamed, because of the lock of white-grey hair at the front of his head) appeared in the Administration's box all the dancers were aware that a highly critical eye was on them. But Kchessinskaya was a dancer of the old regime, and it was from among the young that Diaghilev was eventually going to select the dancers and choreographers with whom he wished to astonish the West. These were Tamara Karsavina, Anna Pavlova and Vaslav Nijinsky, and the choreographer and dancer Michel Fokine. Fokine in

Anna Pavlova, aged 15

particular was growing more and more impatient with the way in which ballet, as danced at St Petersburg, was divorced from life and more and more anxious to bring a breath of fresh air into the antiquated proceedings of the Maryinsky.

For the moment, Diaghilev concerned himself primarily with art and with exhibitions. There was the second *World of Art* exhibition in 1900; another, of Russian painting, in the Academy of Arts in 1901; a monumental book on the 18th-century Russian portrait-painter Levitsky, which won the gold medal of the Imperial Academy of Science; and finally the Exhibition of Historical Russian Portraits (nearly 3,000 of them) at the Tauride Palace (built by Catherine the Great for Potemkin) in early 1905. Diaghilev travelled extensively to assemble this vast exhibition, and was responsible for the nine-part catalogue. The Exhibition made an enormous impact on those who saw it and represented Diaghilev's last and greatest project for revealing their own cultural history to the Russians. Now he was ready to tackle the West.

CHAPTER TWO

Triumph in the West

Diaghilev's next enterprise took place in Paris, which he regarded then, and continued to regard, as the artistic capital of the world. This was the exhibition of Russian Art at the Salon d'Automne in 1906. It presented a summary of Russian art from icon painting to the work of contemporary artists, and made a great impression on Parisian cultural society. The President of the enterprise was the Grand Duke Vladimir, and among the *Présidents d'honneur* was Comtesse Greffulhe, one of the most important hostesses in Paris, married to a rich banker, the original (or one of them) of Proust's Duchesse de Guermantes, and, artistically speaking, a power in the land. Through the *Société des Concerts Français*, of which she was President, she had been instrumental in introducing the work of Mahler to the Parisian audience, and Diaghilev succeeded in interesting her in the idea of a festival of Russian music.

Throughout his career in the theatre Diaghilev made great use of influential patrons, and female ones in particular. Comtesse Greffulhe was later joined by Misia Sert, the Princesse de Polignac and Chanel. In England there were the Marchioness of Ripon, her daughter Lady Juliet Duff, and Lady Cunard. These ladies, together with, in due course, the King of Spain and Princess Charlotte and Prince Pierre of Monaco, were useful to him socially and financially and gave the ballet a cachet which, to him and at the time, was very important. Diaghilev's last protégé, the composer Igor Markevitch, wrote that for the Russian impresario smart premières in the salons of society hostesses were essential: 'In every important city he knew at least one lady whom he turned into the queen of a hive. He went from one of them to the other humming the good news and urging them to turn it into as efficacious a honey as possible.' In other words, with the contrivance of these ladies Diaghilev made judicious use of fashionable musical receptions to prepare the way for his new creations. It was a technique which served him well to the end of his career.

At this time Diaghilev met Gabriel Astruc, a music publisher and concert promoter who was interested in new and unusual music. He was later to build the Théâtre des Champs-Elysées. Astruc agreed to arrange five concerts of Russian music at the Paris Opéra in the late spring of 1907. These were to introduce a great deal of unfamiliar Russian music to the French public, and to present outstanding Russian artists, notably Chaliapine. Rimsky-Korsakov conducted (not, in fact, very well, but the Paris audience liked his work and gave him a good reception); Rachmaninov played his Piano Concerto No 2; music by Glinka, Glazunov and Scriabin was played; but it was probably the singers

Tamara Karsavina (second from left) with Lady Juliet Duff, the Marchioness of Ripon and two unidentified men

Felia Litvinne and above all Chaliapine who made the strongest impression in scenes from *Prince Igor*, *Khovanshchina* and *Boris Godunov*. The way was clear for a season of Russian opera in 1908. This took the form of peformances of *Boris Godunov* with Chaliapine in the title role. The first night, in the presence of three Russian Grand Dukes and the French President, was an enormous triumph.

It was through *Boris* that Diaghilev met Misia Godebska, partly Polish in origin, and better-known to artistic history as Misia Sert. She had been mar-

ried first to Thadée Natanson, co-founder of *La Revue Blanche*, and then to the very wealthy newspaper tycoon and entrepreneur Alfred Edwards, and was now starting her long relationship with the Catalan painter José-Maria Sert. Misia expressed enormous and extravagant admiration for *Boris*, and she became Diaghilev's closest woman friend and one of his most useful and loyal allies. As Misia's biographers, Arthur Gold and Robert Fizdale, say:

'Generosity and cruelty, wild enthusiasm and deadly boredom, arrogance and humility, all the heights and depths of the slavic temperament possessed them both.

It was precisely Misia's slavic qualities which made their great friendship possible, for Diaghilev was never to have a true affinity with anyone who was not a Slav. There was no doubt in Misia's mind that she valued her friendship with Diaghilev above all others. Diaghilev for his part said that the only woman he could ever have imagined marrying was Misia – that she was his closest woman friend, the sister he never had.'

Diaghilev had been thinking about bringing the Imperial Ballet to Paris since 1906, and by 1908

Coco Chanel wearing a 'Chanel' suit, c1929

his wish to do so had crystallized into determination. But he still did not feel that Paris would accept evenings composed entirely of ballets. Richard Buckle points out that many people in the ballet world subsequently claimed to have urged Diaghilev to take this very important step. Among them was Astruc, who wrote as follows in the 1930 special number of *La Revue Musicale*, which was devoted to the *Ballets Russes*:

> 'You seem to love the dance, Sergei said to me. What a pity that you have not been to St Petersburg . . . In France, dance is not honoured as it is in Russia. It is an incomplete art here, because you have fine women dancers but you do not know what a male dancer can be. In Russia, they too are stars.'

In Astruc's account, Diaghilev went on to talk lyrically about Nijinsky, Pavlova and Fokine. So impressed was the Frenchman that he told Diaghilev that these great artists *must* come to Paris the following year. However accurate Astruc's account of this conversation may have been, a contract was indeed signed, Astruc to be in charge of the administration and Diaghilev taking responsibility for the financial side.

PLANNING A PARIS SEASON

During the previous four years or so there had been important developments within the Imperial Ballet and it was these that now led to Diaghilev's increased eagerness to bring Russian ballet to the West in general and Paris in particular. The young American dancer Isadora Duncan appeared in St Petersburg towards the end of 1904, and her naturalism and simplicity had a great effect on Fokine's ideas, as did her use of the music of Chopin, for instance. Indeed, after the heavy intricacies of the Imperial Ballet, many of the young dancers and artists connected with the ballet took readily to the seemingly artless quality of Duncan's work. At a charity double bill at the Maryinsky in February 1907 Fokine created *Chopiniana*, the first version of what was to become a very different ballet, *Les Sylphides*, but already ideas derived at least in part from Duncan were bearing fruit. The C sharp minor waltz – the only number to be carried forward into *Les Sylphides* – was danced by Pavlova. When the ballet was revised and renamed the directly dramatic element which had existed in *Chopiniana* was removed, all the women were now dressed, as Pavlova had been, in the style of the Romantic ballet of Taglioni's day, and the work became the gentle ballet of mood which we still know. But the very gentleness of the final product is apt to make us forget the great originality of Fokine's conception: the *corps de ballet* is hardly an ensemble at all, more a group of individual soloists working together in carefully balanced harmony.

Two further ballets created by Fokine at this time were also chosen to form part of the dance repertoire which Diaghilev and his collaborators – among others the painters Bakst, Benois and Serov, Walter Nuvel and the composer Nicolas Tcherepnine, Fokine, and Diaghilev's new *régisseur* Sergei Grigoriev – proposed to show to Paris. These were *Le Pavillon d'Armide* and *Une Nuit d'Egypte*, though the latter in particular was drastically remodelled, especially on the musical front, before Diaghilev was satisfied with it. *Le Pavillon d'Armide* was a true collaboration between the choreographer, the composer (Tcherepnine) and the designer (Benois), and this notion too was a complete novelty: it was also the first appearance of the balletic aesthetic which was to dominate all Diaghilev's work for the stage – the Wagnerian idea of the *Gesamtkunstwerk*.

In an article published well over 20 years later, the writer Emile Henriot summed it up in these words:

'[All the elements] were combined and melted together so intimately that when one remembers them one cannot separate one part of these beautiful spectacles from the rest . . . The Ballets Russes *were the triumph of unity, and that, I think, is the great law of all classical creation.'*

It goes without saying that Diaghilev did not always attain this kind of perfection, and many later works surpassed *Le Pavillon d'Armide* in power and invention, but it was the first sign of what was to come.

Le Pavillon d'Armide is a story of a Gobelin tapestry that comes to life, bringing the beautiful Armida before the captivated Vicomte René, who promptly falls in love with her. The plot provided the opportunity for a great deal of spectacular dancing, and there were excellent roles for Pavlova and Nijinsky. The first performance (in November 1907) was a success, but not the outright triumph it was to be in Paris.

Une Nuit d'Egypte was a very different and somewhat lurid affair, set in the Egypt of Cleopatra's time (Diaghilev renamed it *Cléôpatre*). A young nobleman called Amoun is in love with Ta-Hor, a temple attendant, but is so dazzled by the beauty of the Queen that in order to spend one night with her he consents to take poison the following morning. Ta-Hor is left mourning her dead lover. It sounds preposterous enough today, in all truth, but Diaghilev's instinct was right: spectacularly presented and magnificently danced, it had the ingredients of yet another huge success. The problem was Arensky's music, which Diaghilev did not care for at all. To the astonishment of his collaborators, he cut the existing score to ribbons and introduced music, mostly of an Oriental flavour, composed by, among others, Rimsky-Korsakov, Glinka, Mussorgsky, Glazunov and Tcherepnine.

Diaghilev was beginning to sign contracts with his dancers and singers. He was determined to present Pavlova and Karsavina, and, above all, on the male side, Nijinsky. Diaghilev had seen him dance in *Le Pavillon d'Armide* and *Une Nuit d'Egypte*, and had been overpowered by his brilliance. Then, in the autumn of 1908, Prince Pavel Dmitrievitch Lvov introduced Nijinsky to Diaghilev, who promptly fell in love with the young man. Nijinsky's attitude to this development is uncertain, since he was always mentally unstable and his *Diary*, written some 10 years later, is a notoriously unreliable document. But he would now be presented to the Western public as the dancing genius that he was, and only later did Diaghilev's violently possessive jealousy contribute to the break-up, emotionally and artistically, of the relationship.

ABOVE LEFT: *Lady Cunard*

BELOW LEFT: *Tamara Karsavina in* Le Pavillon d'Armide

Vaslav Nijinsky in Le Pavillon d'Armide

It was a little later that Diaghilev heard Stravinsky's music for the first time, met the composer, and commissioned a Chopin orchestration from him for *Les Sylphides*.

At this stage the plans for the Paris season were very ambitious and were to include four operas and several ballets. But disaster struck on 22 February, 1909, with the death of the Grand Duke Vladimir Alexandrovitch, the main Russian patron of the forthcoming season, who had obtained a substantial subsidy from the Tsar. Diaghilev and also Benois had enemies in St Petersburg, and the very powerful Kchessinskaya now became one of them. Angered by the fact that she was to have only one role (Armida) in Paris, and that she was going to have to share even that, she so arranged matters that the subsidy arranged by the late Grand Duke was withdrawn, and the money for the season vanished. Diaghilev's initial reaction was despair, but this did not last very long. He returned to Paris and induced Astruc to find the money at the French end. Somehow, Astruc did so. Once again the enterprise was viable. 'The impossibilist has his great army on the march,' said Benois of his indomitable friend, but money was to be a problem that haunted Diaghilev all his life.

The Tsar was also being unhelpful in various other ways – Diaghilev would now have to find alternatives to scenery and costumes which he had hoped to borrow, and he was not to be allowed to use the Hermitage Theatre for rehearsals – but nothing was going to stop Diaghilev now. It was in an obscure hall in St Petersburg that Fokine set to work on creating his version of the Polovtsian Dances from *Prince Igor*.

Design by Alexandre Benois for the decor of Le Pavillon d'Armide, *Scene II, Armide's Garden. The ballet was revived for the first Paris season in May 1909, having been first performed at the Maryinsky, St Petersburg in 1907.*

In the French capital Astruc's publicity campaign was being set in motion. The Théâtre du Châtelet, where the Russian performances were to take place, had gone to seed. Diaghilev had it entirely redecorated and had nine rows of stalls taken out so that there would be room for a large orchestra. Telegrams flew backwards and forwards between St Petersburg and Paris. The dancers arrived at the beginning of May, as did Diaghilev, only to tell Astruc that he had run out of money and the Frenchman would have to pay the company out of subscriptions and advance bookings. Astruc gulped, but again made the necessary arrangements. Robert Brussel, music critic of *Le Figaro* and an adviser of Diaghilev's since 1906, printed a series of articles and paragraphs drumming up publicity for the *Ballets Russes*. For the *répétition générale* on 18 May, 1909, Astruc filled the front row of the dress-circle with the prettiest women he could find, mostly actresses, blondes alternating with brunettes. Thereafter the dress-circle was known as the *corbeille* (flower-basket). The audience was of the utmost distinction, social and artistic: aristocrats, high officials, writers, composers, painters, singers and the directors of other theatres, from the USA as well as from France itself. Diaghilev was in Misia Sert's box.

The programme began with *Le Pavillon d'Armide*, which the composer himself conducted. Benois'

RIGHT: *Design for Scenes I and III – The Pavilion – of* Le Pavillon d'Armide

BELOW: *Nicolas Roerich's design for the decor of* Prince Igor, *Act III, The Polovtsian Camp*

FAR RIGHT: *Two of Roerich's designs for the Polovtsian Dances, Act III,* Prince Igor

decor and costumes were, entirely appropriately, in the rococo style, and there was a danger that a Paris audience would find them insipid, despite the fact that they were executed with great taste. But the dancing took care of that: not so much that of Vera Karalli and Michel Mordkine, the principals (Armida and René), good as they were, but that of the far greater dancers taking lesser roles in the *divertissement* section. The atmosphere in the theatre became electric with the *pas de trois* of Karsavina, Baldina and Nijinsky, and Nijinsky's final leap off the stage – spontaneous, according to Karsavina – brought the house down. Nijinsky's solo *variation* produced another ovation, and Karsavina won all hearts with hers. By the time the rest of the ballet, which included a spectacular Buffoons' Dance, came to an end, it was clear that the evening was set to be an immense success.

Any doubts that might conceivably have remained were swept away by the second item in the programme, the Polovtsian Act of *Prince Igor*, with singers, dancers, chorus and orchestra. Roerich's set conjured up the atmosphere of a remote and barbaric Russia, the singing was of great beauty, but it was the now famous Polovtsian Dances which aroused the wildest enthusiasm of the audience. The savage dances of the warriors, led by the phenomenal Adolf Bolm, carried the Parisians away.

The last ballet, a *divertissement* called *Le Festin* to a mixed bag of Russian music by Rimsky-Korsakov, Glinka (including the Caucasian Lezginka from *Ruslan*, already mentioned for its astonishing originality), Tchaikovsky, Glazunov and Mussorgsky, might have come as a disappointment, but it did not. No wonder, when it contained the Blue Bird *pas de deux* from *The Sleeping Beauty*, the first time this celebrated piece was seen in the West, danced with every possible virtuosity by Karsavina and Nijinsky. Curiously, the *pas de deux* was billed as *L'Oiseau de feu*, with the roles reversed, the woman as a bird, the man as a Prince. The evening ended in complete triumph, with the audience pouring on to the stage, eager to see their new favourites at close quarters.

The second programme was an operatic one, the first performance outside Russia of Rimsky-Korsakov's *The Maid of Pskov*, renamed *Ivan the*

ABOVE: *Roerich's design for the decor of the Polovtsian Dances,* Prince Igor

RIGHT: *This is thought to be a drawing of Ida Rubinstein in the title role of* Cléopâtre

Terrible. The Russian decors were much admired, and Chaliapine, as Ivan, impressed as much as he already had as Boris. Later on a second opera, Alexander Serov's *Judith* (now quite forgotten) was given, but the third Russian programme, largely ballet, first given on 2 June, produced a similar effect to that of the first. It began with the first act of *Ruslan and Ludmila*, which was not perhaps as 'Russian' – at least in the obvious sense – as people were now hoping and expecting, but which was enjoyed and praised. Then came *Les Sylphides*, with Pavlova, Karsavina and Nijinsky. The Paris audience had taken Karsavina to their hearts (she had since taken the part of Armida because of a defection in the company): now they saw Pavlova, and were absolutely entranced by her extreme lightness and delicacy.

Pavlova also appeared in the final ballet of the evening, *Cléopâtre*. She danced Ta-Hor, the temple attendant, Fokine was her lover, Amoun, and Karsavina and Nijinsky were slaves. The Queen herself was Ida Rubinstein, a young woman of spectacular beauty from a rich Russian-Jewish family. In time her distinctly limited gifts as a

dancer, actress and speaker would be paraded all over Europe (though not by Diaghilev), but on this occasion Diaghilev's instinct had been perfect. After the first dance of Ta-Hor and Amoun, the Queen's procession came on to the stage, carrying a large sarcophagus. Jean Cocteau described the effect:

'The bearers set the casket down in the middle of the temple, opened its double lid, and from within lifted a kind of mummy, a bundle of veils, which they placed upright on its ivory pattens. Then four slaves began an astonishing manoeuvre. They unwound the first veil, which was red, with silver lotuses and crocodiles; then

the second veil, which was green, with the history of the dynasties in gold filigree; then the third, which was orange with prismatic stripes, and so on . . . The twelfth veil, dark blue, Mme Rubinstein released herself, letting it fall with a sweeping circular gesture. She stood leaning forward, her shoulders slightly hunched like the wings of an ibis; overcome by her long wait, having submitted in her dark coffin, as had we, to the intolerable and sublime music of her cortège . . . She was wearing a small blue wig, from which a short golden braid hung down on either side of her face. There she stood, unswathed, eyes vacant, cheeks pale, lips parted . . . and as she confronted the stunned audience, she was too beautiful, like a too potent oriental fragrance.'

For a time *Cléopâtre* was the most popular ballet of all, according to Benois, and Bakst's setting – his first work to be seen in Paris, apart from the Blue Bird costumes – with its giant gods and columns in exotic colours, had an almost immediate effect on clothes, furnishings and decoration, as did *Schéhérazade* the following year.

The fact that it was Jean Cocteau who wrote so lyrical a description of the entrance of Ida Rubinstein is highly significant. Parisian artists and intellectuals were drawn at once into the circle of the *Ballets Russes*, with the active encouragement of Diaghilev. Proust's biographer, George Painter, writes rather sourly that 'the camp-following of artists and intellectuals which formed an indispensable part of the Diaghilev circus was beginning to gather'. The leaders of the homosexual side of Parisian social and artistic life (a powerful group at that time and for a long while afterwards) were especially drawn to the *Ballets Russes*. They included Proust himself, his friend the composer Reynaldo Hahn, Lucien Daudet and Cocteau. Misia Sert's drawing-room in the Rue de Rivoli became the informal headquarters for these friends of the ballet.

But this was by no means the whole story. Diaghilev was in the process of commissioning the ballet *Daphnis and Chloë* from Ravel, and wanted something from Debussy as well. Painter is closer to the mark, perhaps, when he speaks of the 'incessant cross-fertilization, devised by the strange and cunning genius of Diaghilev, by which the marvellous organism of the *Ballets Russes* grew and ripened'. Diaghilev always looked to the future: he wanted new ideas. There is no way of telling whether he foresaw at this very early stage that there would come a time when the ideas of his first collaborators – Benois, Bakst, Fokine and so on – would cease to be novel, or that France, already his second, would become his first home. But he wanted to interest French writers, artists and composers in his work, just as he wanted to interest fashionable Parisian society, because he needed the help of both groups to maintain his forward impulse. It was Paris that mattered to him above all, as has been mentioned, but a similar process occurred in England, where, for instance, he made use of the Sitwells; and had it not been for the First World War he would no doubt have formed closer ties in Germany and Austria with such figures as Count Harry Kessler and Hugo von Hofmannsthal.

At all events, Proust speaks in *A la recherche du temps perdu* of the 'charming invasion' of the *Ballets Russes* which 'infected Paris with a fever of curiosity

Nijinsky in Le Festin, *1909*

ABOVE: *Costume design by Bakst for the Jewish Dancer in Cléopâtre, 1910*

FAR RIGHT: *Costume design by Bakst for the Satyrs in Cléopatre*

RIGHT: *Marcel Proust*

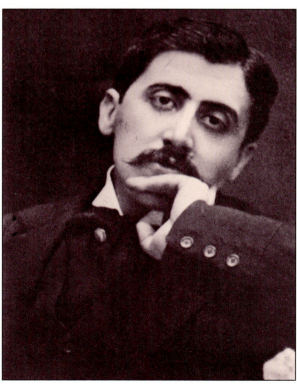

quite as intense as that aroused by the Dreyfus Case'. People in society were avid to meet the dancers, directors, designers, composers, those 'great theatrical innovators who had created a revolution as profound as Impressionism itself'. And such meetings were possible, with Diaghilev's permission and encouragement.

The 1909 season ended on 18 June. It had been an artistic triumph, but there were debts. Astruc was obliged to proceed against Diaghilev, and this created a breach in their relationship which was not completely healed for some time. Diaghilev was hoping for a season at the Opéra in 1910, and unwisely tried to hide this from Astruc. This led to further ill-feeling, as Astruc was making arrangements for a season with Caruso, Toscanini and the Metropolitan Opera at the Châtelet in June 1910, and this would inevitably clash with the proposed Russian season. Through the good offices of various friends, the two men reached an accommodation before the end of the year.

Back in Russia, Diaghilev set about making arrangements for the Paris season. This meant raising money and creating new ballets. One of these was to be completely Russian in every sense: a Russian story, Russian music, and Russian sets. The subject finally decided on was that of the magic Firebird who rescues the victims of the demonic Kastchei the Immortal. Diaghilev asked the composer Liadov for the music. Liadov was a composer of delicate, beautifully turned miniatures (*The Enchanted Lake*, *Kikimora*, the *Russian Folk Tunes*), and he might well have written something very charming. But when Diaghilev discovered after

some time that all Liadov had done was to buy music paper he gave the commission to the virtually unknown Stravinsky. Thus it was through Diaghilev and the *Ballets Russes* that possibly the greatest composer of our century burst upon the Western European public.

It was also decided to take *Giselle* to Paris, mainly as a vehicle for Pavlova (who in the end did not dance it), though Diaghilev, rightly, had grave doubts as to whether it would interest the French audience. There was also to be a ballet to Rimsky-Korsakov's symphonic poem *Schéhérazade* and a *divertissement* called *Les Orientales*, to a mixed collection of music, chosen by Diaghilev himself, on similar lines to the scores of *Cléopâtre* and *Le Festin*. One more new ballet was needed. Fokine had made a chamber ballet to Schumann's *Carnaval* for a Shrove Tuesday ball in St Petersburg on 5 March. Diaghilev did not expect much of it but took it into his repertoire all the same. He now had enough new work for the season.

COULD BALLET SUCCEED WITHOUT OPERA?

The Company opened its Berlin season on 20 May, 1910 and scored an immediate success with *Carnaval*, in which the very young Lydia Lopokova made her first appearance outside Russia. But it remained to be seen what would happen in Paris. The ballet was on its own – there was no opera. Pavlova had other engagements. The first night at the Paris Opéra was on 4 June, and after a *divertissement* the Paris audience had its first sight of *Carnaval*. This went down well enough, with Fokine, Fokina, Lopokova and other talented dancers in the cast. Then the curtain rose on *Schéhérazade*.

Paris had been waiting impatiently for a year for the return of the Russians, but the new ballet surpassed their expectations. The orgy of the harem women with their Negro slaves and the final bloody vengeance of the Shah were a spectacle of a kind never seen before, in Paris or anywhere else for that matter. Ida Rubinstein, so striking in *Cléopâtre*, made an equal though very different impression as Zobeida, not least in her last moments of life. 'She sits utterly still while slaughter takes place around her,' wrote Fokine; 'death approaches her, but not the horror nor the feel of it. She majestically awaits her fate . . .' Nijinsky as the Golden Slave had perhaps the greatest of all his roles. 'He is pleased with himself, like a cat,' said Fokine, when coaching another dancer in the role, and this feline quality, combined with tremendous energy and enormous soft jumps, drew paeans of praise from all who witnessed the ballet. As to the set . . . Here is an extract from Richard Buckle's description:

> 'Not form, but colour reigned, and its reign was as debauched as that of Heliogabalus. An unheard-of violence of peacock-green and blue was the main theme (which gave the jeweller Cartier the idea of setting sapphires and emeralds together for the first time since the Moghul Emperors), but this was defied by the subsidiary theme of coral-red and rose-pink. Against

LEFT: *Maurice Ravel*

ABOVE: *Jean Cocteau in 1929*

ABOVE: Carnaval, *from a group of studies of Ballets Russes productions by Georges Barbier*

ABOVE RIGHT: *Michel Fokine and his wife Vera Fokina in* Carnaval

RIGHT: *Nijinsky as the Golden Slave in* Schéhérazade, *Paris 1910*

this chromatic jungle, with its patches of light and shadowy depths, stood out the royal blues and crimsons of the turbaned brother kings, the green and pink Odalisques who began the drama . . .'

Proust, who was present with Reynaldo Hahn and the poet and art critic Jean-Louis Vaudoyer, astonished by the 'dazzling green tent with shadowy blue doors and a vast orange carpet,' said 'I never saw anything so beautiful'. Harold Acton wrote later of:

'The thunder and lightning of negroes in rose and amber; . . . the fierce orgy of clamorous caresses; death in long-drawn spasms to piercing violins. Rimsky-Korsakov painted the tragedy; Bakst hung it with emerald curtains and silver lamps and carpeted it with rugs from Bokhara and silken cushions. Nijinsky and Karsavina made it live' (Karsavina later took over the role of Zobeida).

In fact the ballet, quite rightly, went to everyone's head, including the heads of couturiers, interior

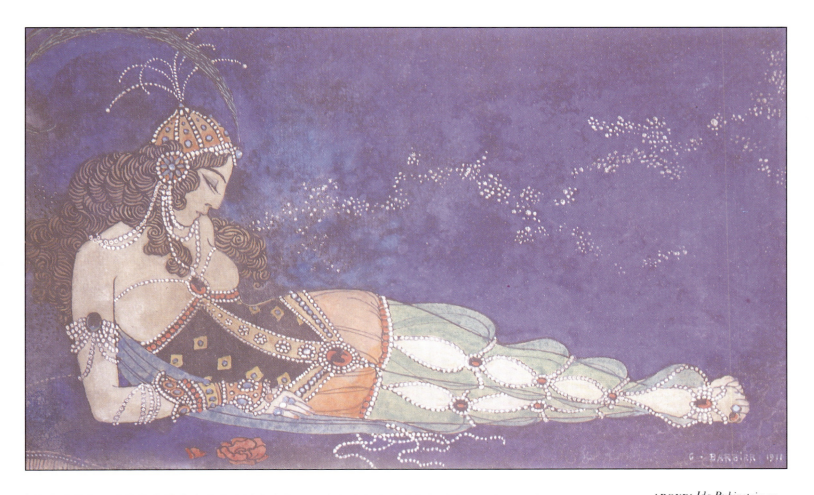

ABOVE: *Ida Rubinstein as Zobeida in* Schéhérazade, *by Georges Barbier, 1911*

LEFT: *Tamara Karsavina as Zobeida in* Schéhérazade

Bakst's design for the Bayadère costume, Schéhérazade, *1910*

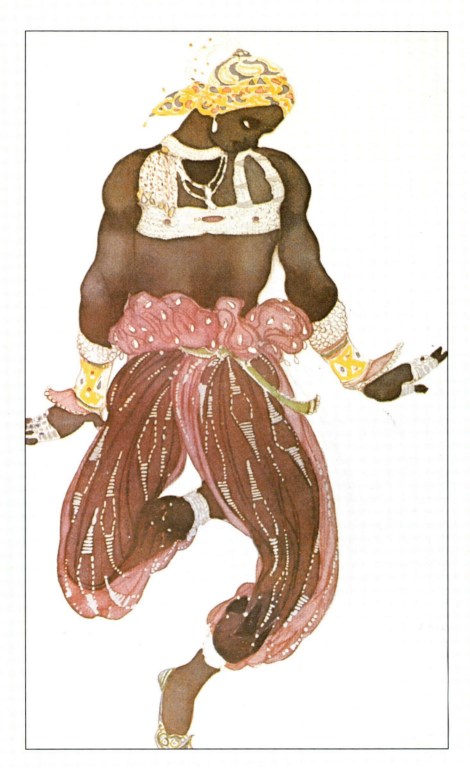

Bakst's design for the Golden
Slave's costume, Schéhérazade

decorators, fabric designers and jewellers. Paul Poiret was only one of many to introduce violent colours and Eastern patterns into the clothes he designed. Drawing-rooms were soon piled with silk cushions in imitation of Bakst. This invasion of orientalia started in Paris but soon spread outward all over Western Europe.

Diaghilev now asked Cocteau and Hahn to devise their own oriental ballet for him, with a leading role for Nijinsky. This was *Le Dieu bleu*. *Schéhérazade*, however, was an uncommonly hard act to follow, and it will be seen that the two Frenchmen did not altogether succeed.

Even with Karsavina and Nijinsky, *Giselle* was little more than a *succès d'estime*. It was – or seemed – too old-fashioned, too gentle, too uneventful for the Parisian audiences: pure cold water after the heady cocktail of *Schéhérazade*, and the audience was in no mood for pure cold water. They wanted violent excitement. They were not to be disappointed, for on 25 June Diaghilev gave them *The Firebird*.

Karsavina danced the Firebird, Fokine, who, as usual, was responsible for the choreography, was Prince Ivan, and his wife Vera Fokina was the beautiful Tsarevna. In the ballet's first scene the Prince captures the mysterious Firebird, who obtains her release only by giving her captor a feather which he can use to call on her in moments of peril. This happens when Ivan falls in love with the beautiful Tsarevna and into the power of the evil monster Kastchei. At the height of the 'Infernal Dance' of Kastchei's followers the Firebird appears and puts the demons to sleep. Ivan smashes the egg which has Kastchei's soul in it, and Ivan and the Tsarevna are married and crowned.

This was another huge success, and Stravinsky's career was launched. Diaghilev introduced him to Debussy, who was complimentary (though, later, when he got to know Stravinsky, he remarked, 'Well, one has to start with *something*'). The only slight weakness lay in Alexander Golovine's sets (something Diaghilev put right when he had the ballet redesigned by Gontcharova in 1926), but this in no way affected the success of the production with the public. The evening was completed by *Les Orientales*, which included a Siamese dance for Nijinsky in a striking Bakst costume.

After two appearances in Brussels, followed by two extra performances at the Paris Opéra, the 1910 season was over. It had not been a financial disaster, partly because Diaghilev had not brought a Russian orchestra and he had not tried to present any opera. Clearly seasons of ballet alone were artistically and financially viable.

Diaghilev perceived that he had an enormous asset in Stravinsky, though he could not have foreseen that the composer would eventually write another seven ballets for him, most of them masterpieces. Indeed Stravinsky had already had his vision of a girl dancing herself to death before the elders of her tribe – an evocation of pagan Russia which he referred to at this time as *The Great Sacrifice* but which was eventually to become world-famous as *The Rite of Spring*. While developing his musical ideas on this theme he also started work on what he called a *Konzertstück* for piano and orchestra to be called *Petrushka's Cry*. He played parts of this to Diaghilev and Nijinsky when they visited him at Lausanne in September 1910, and Diaghilev at once saw the possibility of a ballet to be set within the frame of the Butter Week Fair at St Petersburg.

If Diaghilev had confidence in Stravinsky, he had less in Fokine, whom he was starting to think of as old-fashioned and overly folkloric. The impresario dearly wanted a new choreographer and was beginning to wonder whether Nijinsky had talents

LEFT: *Bakst's costume design for the Head Eunuch in* Schéhérazade

ABOVE: *Tamara Karsavina in* The Firebird

in that direction. Benois, a touchy man at the best of times, had been proving unusually difficult of late, though Bakst, the darling of Parisian audiences, could be relied on to brim over with sensational pictorial inventions. All in all, there was every reason to proceed with future seasons, not only in Paris but in other capitals like London, but to do this as he wished, Diaghilev now wanted a company over which he could have complete control and which would dance all the year, apart from holidays: to have dancers from the Imperial Theatres in what were supposed to be *their* holidays would no longer serve.

Accordingly, Diaghilev began to lure dancers away from the Imperial Theatres and sign them up for his own company. He was lucky to secure Adolf Bolm, who had made such an impression in *Prince Igor*, and Karsavina, now a prima ballerina, could

BELOW: *Costume design by Natalie Gontcharova for* The Firebird, *1926*

RIGHT: *Nijinsky in* Les Orientales *costume by Jacques-Emile Blanche*

combine dancing at the Maryinsky with dancing for Diaghilev. Nijinsky was much more of a problem: he was not free to leave the Imperial Theatres, but chance (or was it?) came to Diaghilev's aid.

Chance took the unexpected form of Nijinsky's costume (or rather partial lack of it) when dancing his first Albrecht in *Giselle* at the Maryinsky in the presence of the Dowager Empress Marie Feodorovna, Alexander III's widow, on 5 February, 1911. There are conflicting accounts of what caused the trouble, and since there are no surviving members of the audience it is impossible to be sure. Romola Nijinsky simply says that the dancer omitted to wear his jockstrap, but this is quite out of the question. Such an action would be unthinkable in London, Paris or New York now, let alone in St Petersburg in 1911: a dancer who was so foolish as to do this would not only look obscene but would be courting physical injury. What appears to have happened is that Nijinsky opted to wear the Act I costume that Benois had designed for Paris. This was composed of tights and a tunic with a skirt over the thighs. Diaghilev had had the skirt somewhat shortened, and the dancer did not wear the trunks over the tights that were customary in ballets of this type in Russia at the time (and which were still disfiguring the male dancers' line when the Bolshoi came to the West for the first time 45 years later).

The result shocked the assistant director, who tried to get Nijinsky to modify it, but the dancer refused and went on. It was said that the Dowager Empress had also been shocked, but even if she had been she was hardly likely to have said so, at least in public. Whoever instigated the trouble, he (or she, for it may have been Kchessinskaya) played straight into Diaghilev's hands. The next day Nijinsky was ordered to apologize or resign; he refused to do either, and was sacked. Diaghilev made quite sure that he did not change his mind.

Diaghilev now had his male star, for whom various roles were being created. Nijinsky would obviously incarnate Petrushka. He was already working with his sister Bronislava on an extremely innovatory ballet to the music of Debussy's *Prélude à l'Après-midi d'un faune*, a work which did not see the light of day till 1912. Reynaldo Hahn had now written most of *Le Dieu bleu*, and was entertained royally in St Petersburg in February. Another French enthusiast for the ballet, Jean-Louis Vaudoyer (who had accompanied Proust to the first night of *Schéhérazade*), had been reminded by an episode in *Carnaval* of the famous lines from Théophile Gautier's poem *Le Spectre de la Rose*, so beautifully set to music by Berlioz in his *Nuits d'été*:

Je suis le spectre d'une rose
Que tu portais hier au bal.

This gave him the idea of a short ballet to be set to Weber's *Invitation à la Valse*, orchestrated by Berlioz: a girl, back from her first ball and dreaming nostalgically in an armchair in her bedroom, is visited by the ghost of the rose she wore. Vaudoyer wrote to Bakst to propose the idea. Bakst liked it; so did Diaghilev and Fokine; and work began. Vaudoyer heard no more about it till he received an invitation to the dress rehearsal of the ballet in April 1911 at Monte Carlo. He was naturally delighted: he might have been less so, perhaps, if he had realized that by this ballet alone, rather unjustly, would his own name be remembered.

Arrangements for the first presentation of Diaghilev's own company in the West were now well under way. They were to go first to Monte Carlo; then to Rome; then Paris; and, it was hoped, to London for the season celebrating the Coronation of

George V and Queen Mary. Thus Diaghilev was widening his horizons drastically and setting a pattern for the future.

The performances at Monte Carlo followed on the heels of the usual winter opera season at the *Salle Garnier*, a jewel of a theatre housed within the casino building itself, with a very small auditorium (524 seats only) but a stage and orchestra pit large enough for ambitious ballet performances. Since Diaghilev's day it has always been considered an ideal theatre for ballet, with its combination of luxury, intimacy, *ambiance* and excellent sight lines. The dancers took to Monte Carlo (as well they might have, in those days) and the backstage facilities were good. Morale was thus very high.

Le Spectre de la Rose, the first new ballet of the 1911 season, was a far greater success than Diaghilev had expected or hoped. Bakst's designs were once again very beautiful, notably Nijinsky's costume covered with silk petals, and Karsavina looked ravishing, though she had been given little dancing to do. The ballet was really Nijinsky's. With that

LEFT: *Nijinsky in* Le Spectre de la Rose

FAR LEFT: *Nijinsky and Karsavina in* Le Spectre de la Rose *by Roberto Montenegro, c1914*

BELOW: *Nijinsky and Karsavina in* Le Spectre de la Rose

This lithograph poster by Jean Cocteau, depicting Karsavina in Le Spectre de la Rose, *was used to advertise the first production.*

*Bakst's costume design for the
First Bacchante in* Narcisse

FAR LEFT: *Bakst design for a costume for* Narcisse

LEFT: Petrushka *by Jacques-Emile Blanche, c1911*

BELOW: *Igor Stravinsky with Nijinsky in his Petrushka costume*

extraordinary instinctive artistry (as opposed to intelligence) which he possessed, he had modified Fokine's rather ordinary choreography and contrived to turn himself into a spirit rather than a powerful male dancer in an unusual and indeed potentially disastrous (because potentially ludicrous) costume and situation. The unanimity of reaction prevents us from doubting the miraculous effect he created, and it is better not to think of recent performances by other male dancers, gifted, certainly, but unable to effect the transformation Nijinsky achieved.

Narcisse, which followed on 26 April, was a collaboration between Fokine, Tcherepnine and Bakst, and was not a great success. Nor did later audiences take greatly to it. The subject of Narcissus and Echo was difficult to convey in interesting choreography. Such praise as it received was reserved for the dancers, Nijinsky in particular. The artist Charles Ricketts, writing about the London performances the following September, said:

'Karsavina surpassed herself as Echo in Narcisse. *She creeps on to the stage, enamoured of Narcisse, and approaches silently, hiding behind trees; she dances in a trance and sinks at Nijinsky's feet at the end of each musical phrase. He leaps like a faun, with such rare clothing on that Duchesses had to be led out of the audience, blinded with emotion, and with their diamond tiaras all awry.'*

*Costume design by Benois for
Nijinsky as Petrushka, 1911*

From Monte Carlo the company proceeded to Rome for a short season, at which no new works were presented. Fokine was busy rehearsing *Petrushka* for Paris. The first novelty at the Châtelet Theatre was *Carnaval*, with a new cast including Nijinsky, Karsavina and Bolm. This was followed by *Narcisse*, *Le Spectre de la Rose*, and the so-called submarine act of Rimsky-Korsakov's *Sadko*, with choreography by Fokine and sets and costumes by Boris Anisfeld. *Petrushka* followed on 13 June and surpassed even *The Firebird* in the estimation of the audience. Benois had set the ballet in the St Petersburg of his own childhood, the 1870s, the two outer *tableaux* showing the seething crowds of the pre-Lent fair, while the two inner scenes took place respectively in Petrushka's cell and in the Moor's quarters. Stravinsky's score astonished the public, but, as so often happens, they were able to accept in the theatre music that would have baffled or even offended them in the concert hall (this was not always to occur, as will be seen). The great Pierre Monteux, at the beginning of his long career, secured a fine performance of a work which was very novel and original at the time (a fact that requires an act of historical imagination for us to realize today, familiar as we are with *Petrushka* from countless gramophone recordings). Nijinsky was overwhelming as the half-human puppet who falls in love with the Ballerina and is killed by the Moor, only to reappear as a ghost on the roof of the booth; Karsavina was the Ballerina, Alexander Orlov the Moor, and the 60-year-old Cecchetti created the role of the Magician. In the light of later events, Nijinsky's portrayal of Petrushka was eventually seen by some as a kind of self-portrait, with Diaghilev, naturally, cast in the role of the Magician, but the comparison was unhelpful: Svengali and Trilby are better left in the fictional world from which they sprang.

The triumphant première had not been without difficulties, of which the audience, happily, was unaware, except for a 20-minute delay between the lowering of the house lights and the rise of the curtain, which, not unnaturally, made them restive. This was *not* due to last-minute arguments about tempi between Stravinsky and Monteux, nor the fact that the dancers were complaining that the stage was cluttered with props, nor even that Fokine was still adding touches to the final scene. No: it was the costumier, threatening to withhold the costumes if he was not paid at once. Diaghilev was obliged to go to Misia Sert's box and ask her for 4,000 francs then and there. 'In those happy days one's chauffeur was always waiting,' as Misia wrote later, and off she went. Fortunately the Châtelet is not very far from the rue de Rivoli, and so the show

Costume designs by Benois for The Guardian of the Peace *(below) and a Young Peasant dressed as an Old Man (above) in* Petrushka

Ballets Russes

ABOVE: *Tamara Karsavina as The Doll in* Petrushka *and (above right) a painted plaster statuette of her in that role by Seraphin Soudbinine.*

FAR RIGHT: *Costume for the Blue God in* Le Dieu bleu, *designed by Bakst*

could proceed. Last-minute financial crises of this kind continued to be a feature of Diaghilev's life to the end.

The *Ballets Russes* had conquered Paris for the third time; now they were to face the very different London audience. They were to open at Covent Garden on 21 June and perform as part of the Coronation Gala programme on 26 June. This latter honour was largely due to the influence of the Marchioness of Ripon (formerly Lady de Grey), a patroness of the arts since the 1890s who, as mentioned earlier (p. 20), was to become a great support to Diaghilev, as was, later, her daughter, Lady Juliet Duff. She had seen Russian ballet in St Petersburg and Paris, and it was her enthusiasm which led Joseph and Thomas Beecham to present Diaghilev's company at Covent Garden. The first programme consisted of *Le Pavillon d'Armide*, *Carnaval* and the *Prince Igor* dances, and the audience loved them all. So did the press. *The Times* said that 'it has been obvious for some years that Russians are the ideal dancers of the world'. Others spoke of a revelation, and so it must have been: there had been no dancing of this standard in London since the days of Taglioni and Grisi. Though the audience at the Coronation Gala could not, because of the presence of the King and Queen, applaud with the wildness that is normal today on the rare occasions when there is anything to justify it, they too were obviously captivated. Diaghilev's company had never performed before so brilliant an audience, at least in the social sense. Diaghilev wrote that there were almost as many maharajahs as roses in the theatre, a trifling exaggeration which can be forgiven him in his triumph.

A further London season at Covent Garden was arranged for October, with not only Karsavina but Pavlova and (perhaps somewhat surprisingly, all things considered) Kchessinskaya. Nijinsky was to dance with all three. Even with Karsavina and Nijinsky, *Giselle* left the Covent Garden audience fairly cold, but *Schéhérazade* redeemed the evening. Pavlova, in her last appearances with Diaghilev's company, was recognized as a great dancer but no more than Karsavina could she arouse any enthusiasm for the ballet itself. A shortened version of *Le*

Bakst's design for the Young Rajah's costume in Le Dieu bleu

*Bakst's costume design for the
Blue God in* Le Dieu bleu

ABOVE: *Nijinsky as the Blue God in* Le Dieu bleu

RIGHT: *Bakst's design for Karsavina as The Fiancée in* Le Dieu bleu

FAR RIGHT: *Karsavina as The Fiancée*

Lac des Cygnes fared little better, and in this case the ballerina was not much liked either: whatever she may have written herself, Kchessinskaya did not greatly appeal to the public. It was the Fokine ballets that people loved.

During the winter of 1911–12 there were short seasons in Paris, Berlin, Dresden, Vienna and Budapest. In Vienna, Diaghilev had discussions with the poet and librettist Hugo von Hofmannsthal about a possible Richard Strauss ballet for Nijinsky. In Budapest a young Hungarian, Romola de Pulszky, saw Nijinsky for the first time: a seemingly unimportant event which was to have calamitous results. Seldom can so fundamentally unimportant and untalented a person have created such disruption in artistic matters.

In mid-March the company arrived at Monte Carlo and started rehearsals. There were to be four new ballets in 1912, the premières of all of them being kept for Paris. These were *Le Dieu bleu* and *Daphnis and Chloë*, already mentioned, and another Fokine ballet to the symphonic poem *Thamar* by Balakirev, together with Nijinsky's ballet to the *Prélude à l'Après-midi d'un faune*. The last of these, while brief and with a cast of only eight, needed a great many rehearsals, because Nijinsky was asking the dancers to move in a way which was unfamiliar to them and which conflicted with many aspects of their training. *The Rite of Spring* was going to carry this process a great deal further. There were quarrels over rehearsal time, and Fokine, who felt he was being pushed aside and neglected, intimated his intention of leaving after the season in Paris was over. Diaghilev made no attempt to stop him, and Stravinsky was positively glad to see him go. The Monte Carlo season passed without incident and without novelties.

Of the new ballets to be seen at the Châtelet, *Le Dieu bleu* was first performed on 13 May, 1912. The somewhat preposterous 'Hindu' plot dreamed up by Cocteau concerns a young man who is about to become a priest of the temple. A girl who loves him tries to make him change his mind, and for this the priests condemn her to death. During the night monsters torment her, but first the Goddess and then the Blue God himself (Krishna) appear and save the lovers. The first disappointment about the new offering was the music. Reynaldo Hahn was a good musician and during his lifetime wrote many excellent songs and a number of accomplished light operas and operettas. But he was simply incapable of portraying steamy events in India, and it is surprising that anyone ever thought that he would be. Nor, apparently, was Fokine's choreography particularly inventive, apart from a solo dance for Nijinsky. Bakst, on the other hand, had excelled

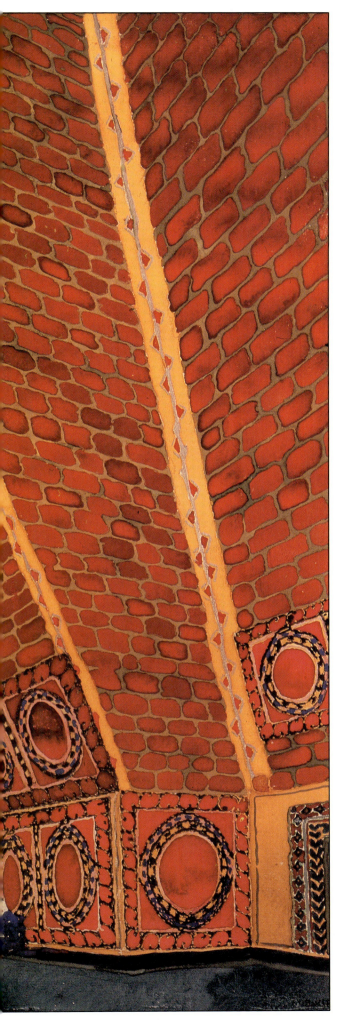

Bakst's dramatic design for the set of Thamar, *1912*

himself with a set depicting a pool dominated by orange rocks 'carved into the heads of gods, beneath a boiling sky of ultramarine' (Buckle). The costumes were white with a fantastic variety of patterns superimposed on them. Nijinsky was given a yellow costume and a gold head-dress, and his skin was painted blue. His appearance and dancing, together with the superb set, ensured a degree of success for the ballet, but there was no point in pretending that it was another *Schéhérazade* in its impact.

Thamar, another exercise in exoticism, followed on 20 May. If *Le Dieu bleu* had been Nijinsky's ballet, this was Karsavina's. She played Thamar, Queen of Georgia, who lures young men into her palace by waving a scarf and, when they have made love to her, has them thrown into the river below. Bakst had once again done wonders. Above the piles of cushions on the stage rose the interior of a vast tower in reddish-purple. The violent, dramatic set was a perfect background (if so striking a design could be described as such) for the savage action. But once again the music was a problem. Not that Balakirev's symphonic poem is not good: far from it – it is one of the great masterpieces of Russian music. Writing about *Thamar*, Constant Lambert put his finger on the problem by comparing the ballet with *Schéhérazade*:

'I am not alone in considering Balakirev's work greatly superior from the purely musical point of view, and I expect many will agree with me in preferring Fokine's choreography and Bakst's decor in Thamar *to their work in* Schéhérazade, *considered as separate artistic elements. Yet* Schéhérazade *is to me the more successful and satisfying ballet of the two, for the simple reason that the music has the direct two-dimensional quality of present action, while Balakirev's work has the more subtle quality of imagined or recollected action. The success is all the more remarkable when we remember that the scenario of* Thamar *follows closely the Lermontov poem around which Balakirev wrote his symphonic poem, while the scenario of* Schéhérazade *has nothing in common with the stories round which Rimsky-Korsakov wrote his symphonic suite. The point, I think, is this: Rimsky-Korsakov's formal outlook being as simple and direct as the narrative methods of the* Arabian Nights *themselves, his music lends itself to any tale of a type similar to those he actually chose to illustrate. Balakirev, on the other hand, approaches his subject with something of the formal subtlety of a Conrad, and hence even the most painstaking realization of his tale does a certain violence to the musical content. There is in* Thamar *none of the obvious physical climax which lends itself so successfully to action in the closing scene of* Schéhérazade. *Instead we are given an emotional summing-up after the action is over. As a result the*

actual murder of the Prince on the stage is too strong an action for the music, while on the other hand the epilogue is choreographically speaking too weak.'
This opinion has been quoted at some length because of its value as the view of a man who knew more than most about ballet in general and music for ballet in particular. All this said, however, *Thamar* was still being danced to admiring audiences in the 1930s, and the part of the Queen was a wonderful role for a number of dancers, notably Lubov Tchernicheva.

NIJINSKY'S SCANDALOUS FAUN

Audiences which adored *Schéhérazade* had no difficulty in accepting *Le Dieu bleu* and *Thamar*: the settings were different, the subjects were different, but the aesthetic was the same. This was very far from being the case with the next ballet to be shown to the public, Nijinsky's *L'Après-midi d'un faune*. Not only was the style of dancing utterly different, but the subject-matter was sexually explicit in a way that no ballet had ever been before. *Schéhérazade* and *Thamar* had certainly been 'about' sex, but in Cocteau's phrase, they had 'known how far to go too far'. The new ballet went a great deal too far for some people. It would have been disingenuous to justify its explicitness by reference to the Mallarmé poem which suggested Debussy's *Prélude*, since while many people professed to admire Mallarmé few could truthfully claim to understand him. His style saw to that, and still does, for that matter. In any case an action described, especially in tortuous verse, on the printed page can never have the impact of the same action played out physically before one.

What was all the fuss about? The programme notes read:

'A faun dozes,
Nymphs tease him,
A forgotten scarf satisfies his dream.
The curtain descends so that the poem can begin in everyone's memory.' In the ballet, the Faun sees seven nymphs. He is attracted to one of them, who undresses to bathe. He tries to catch her, and fails, but as she runs away she abandons a scarf. The Faun takes it, goes back to the rock on which he was lying when the ballet started, lies down on the scarf, and masturbates to the point of orgasm. This, of course, is what caused the trouble, and, baldly described as it just has been, it can certainly sound somewhat repellent. But, as will be seen, a great artist like Rodin did not find it so.

The choreographic style of the ballet was also most disconcerting. Nijinsky had chosen to make Debussy's beautifully fluid score the basis of a series of angular, unclassical movements. Throughout, the dancers were seen entirely in profile, like a Greek frieze, except for their torsos, which faced the audience. Their movements were made on the flat of the foot, knees bending only a little. To dance in this way was of course entirely foreign to the dancers portraying the seven nymphs, and it has been stated that 120 rehearsals had been necessary to achieve the desired effect.

About the sets and costumes there could be little doubt. Bakst's pastoral landscape was one of his most beautiful. The nymphs wore long pleated gauze tunics, cream with blue and green motifs painted on them. As Martin Howe wrote:

'Nijinsky was dressed in coffee-coloured tights on which were disposed brown patches that so overlapped from tights to flesh that the general effect was to merge the human with the animal. This effect was heightened by the lengthening of his ears with flesh-coloured wax, two horns which peeped from a gold wig, and a short tail which hung from behind a garland of leaves round his hips.'

ABOVE: *Head of Nijinsky as the faun in* L'Après-midi d'un faune *by Una Troubridge*

LEFT: *Claude Debussy*

Set of photographs by Baron de Meyer of Nijinsky performing L'Après-midi d'un faune *(in one he is shown with Bronislava Nijinska, his sister)*

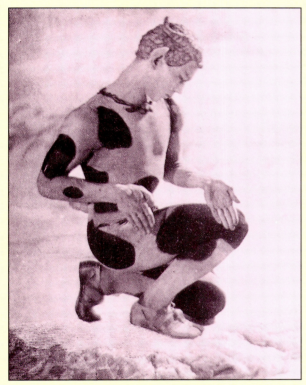

Bakst set for Scene III of
Daphnis and Chloë

Karsavina in Daphnis and Chloë, *1912*

By any criterion, it was one of the most beautiful costumes Bakst or anyone else ever designed.

The question then was: how would the public react firstly to the unfamiliar kind of movement and secondly to the unambiguous suggestion of onanism? There is no doubt at all about what Nijinsky meant to convey. There was a tendency at one point to say that it was all a mistake, and that all the dancer had done was to put his hand down his body to adjust some glass ornaments that were hurting him. Orgasm was the only logical way to end the episode, even if the action was flying in the face of the music (which it was). Romola Nijinsky sensibly (for once) described it as 'an everyday act of fetishism'. On the other hand Nijinsky wrote defensively that 'when I composed this ballet I was not thinking of perversity'. Indeed no, for if masturbation is perverse few men would escape the charge. The basic question was, and is, whether it was aesthetically – or morally – right to show it on stage.

Diaghilev invited the press and various friends of the *Ballets Russes* to a midday rehearsal, with champagne and caviar, on 28 May. According to Fokine, who is not necessarily to be trusted because of his dislike of Nijinsky and his work, there was no applause at all. In view of this it was decided to repeat the ballet (after all, it lasts only about 12 minutes) on the grounds that so novel a work needed to be seen more than once. After the second performance there was some applause. At the first night on 29 May there was a mixture of applause and booing. Some supporters, however, called for an encore, and Diaghilev willingly gave it. But that was by no means that.

There was praise from several quarters, but not from Gaston Calmette, the editor of the right-wing *Figaro*. Calmette took over from his music critic Robert Brussel, who, as has been mentioned, was a friend of the *Ballets Russes*, and himself wrote a violent attack on the new work. It may have been a case of genuine moral indignation. More probably it was simply a journalistic wish to cause a scandal. The Russian Embassy thought that it was a veiled attack on French foreign policy – at the time Poincaré and the Russian Ambassador, Isvolsky, were trying to strengthen the ties between France and Russia. At all events Calmette wrote:

'Anyone who mentions the words "art" and "imagination" in the same breath as this production must be laughing at us. This is neither a pretty pastoral nor a work of profound meaning. We are shown a lecherous faun, whose movements are filthy and bestial in their eroticism, and whose gestures are as crude as they are indecent. That is all. And the over-explicit miming of this misshapen beast, loathsome when seen full on, but even more loathsome in profile, was greeted with the booing it deserved.'

Diaghilev's blood was up. He appealed to the sculptor Rodin and the artist Odilon Redon, who had been a friend of Mallarmé, and they promptly wrote letters of support for publication in the press. Odilon Redon stated firmly that his late friend would have adored the ballet. Rodin went much further:

'Form and meaning are indissolubly wedded in his [Nijinsky's] body . . . His beauty is that of antique frescos and sculpture: he is the ideal model, whom one longs to draw and sculpt. When the curtain rises to reveal him reclining on the ground, one knee raised, the pipe at his lips, you would think him a statue; and nothing could be more striking than the impulse with which, at the climax, he lies face down on the scented veil, kissing it and hugging it to him with passionate abandon . . . I wish that such a noble endeavour

should be understood as a whole . . . and that the Théâtre du Châtelet would arrange others [other performances] to which all our artists might come for inspiration and to communicate in beauty.'

The correspondence dragged on for some time, but Calmette had lost. Naturally all Paris was now determined to see what all the furore was about. Houses were full every night, and Diaghilev programmed extra performances of the ballet. He also took the precaution of quietly toning down the ending. This meant that *Daphnis and Chloë*, the last new ballet of the season, received only two performances and no *répétition générale*, which infuriated the choreographer, Fokine, and the composer, Ravel. Bakst's sets were again very beautiful. The score is recognized as one of the greatest written in the 20th century. Nijinsky danced Daphnis and Karsavina the shepherdess Chloë, who is stolen from her lover by pirates and rescued by the intervention of the God Pan. But the work did not quite come off. Why? Was it because Daphnis is a limp kind of hero, content to lie in a swoon while the God, as it were, does his work for him? Was Fokine's choreographic imagination failing? For whatever reason the reception was more polite than enthusiastic on the first night, 8 June, 1912.

It is curious to note that when Frederick Ashton made his version of *Daphnis and Chloë* for the Sadler's Wells Ballet in 1951 he did not entirely succeed either. Ashton's choreography for Fonteyn as Chloë was totally convincing, and the opening *Danse religieuse*, based very intelligently on modern Greek folk dance, was one of his most beautiful conceptions, but the two great group dances, the *Danse guerrière* of the pirates and the Bacchanal (*Danse générale*), though they did not actually defeat Ashton. lacked something. Perhaps it was because both numbers, characterized by cumulative excitement, continually building, are very hard for a choreographer to match. For whatever reason, this episode from Longus's charming little tale has never made a satisfactory stage work.

Without Fokine, who had been as good as his word and resigned, the company opened in London on 12 June. Once again they were at Covent Garden, with Thomas Beecham conducting some of the works. The success was total. After a short season at Deauville, the company had no more engagements till Cologne at the end of October.

Three new ballets, all destined in one way or another for Nijinsky, were now in preparation. The first was *The Rite of Spring*, the second was the Hugo von Hofmannsthal/Richard Strauss project, at this stage called *Joseph in Egypt*, and the third was *Jeux*. Debussy, who had disliked Nijinsky's treatment of his *Prélude à l'Après-midi d'un faune*, had at first refused to write a score whose subject, it seemed, was to be a game of tennis in a garden, but Diaghilev doubled his fee and he set to work. One only hopes that he was paid in full and on time.

The autumn season took the company successively to Cologne, Frankfurt, Munich and Berlin. At this time Diaghilev and Nijinsky visited for the second time Jacques-Emile Dalcroze's School of Eurhythmics at Hellerau to see whether Dalcroze's system of analysis would help in the staging of the new ballets that were planned, notably *The Rite of Spring*, which was obviously going to be very difficult to mount. As a result, Diaghilev hired the services of one of Dalcroze's pupils, Miriam Ramberg, better-known in ballet history under the illustrious name of Marie Rambert.

After Berlin there were performances in Budapest, Vienna, Prague, Leipzig, Dresden, London and Lyons, before the company reassembled at Monte Carlo in March. During the Vienna season the Hungarian Romola de Pulszky had succeeded in persuading Diaghilev to allow her to travel with the *Ballets Russes* and study their work. It was Nijinsky that she was interested in studying, of course.

The Paris season was to take place at Astruc's new theatre, the Théâtre des Champs-Elysées, in the avenue Montaigne. The new ballets were *Jeux*, *The Rite of Spring* and a version of Florent Schmitt's *La Tragédie de Salomé*, to be choreographed by Boris Romanov, whom Diaghilev had recently taken on, and intended as a consolation prize to Karsavina for all the attention that Nijinsky was going to get.

Jeux was first shown to a baffled and indifferent public on 15 May, 1913. The scene is a garden near a tennis court. A tennis ball rolls on to the stage, and a young man with a tennis racquet follows and starts to look for it. Two girls appear, and they all start to flirt with one another in movements suggestive perhaps of tennis or perhaps something else. Their ambiguous goings-on are cut short by another tennis ball, rolling on to the stage like the first. This is the end of the ballet.

As a reflection of modern life (it was supposed to be the first ballet on a contemporary theme) it left a great deal to be desired. In the first place, even in 1913, the idea of a game of tennis for three could not but seem odd – unless it was the impatient fourth, never seen, who sent the second ball on to the stage as a subtle way of suggesting that his companions should abandon their flirtations and get back to the court? In any case, was the ballet really about tennis at all? Nijinsky, writing later in his *Diary*, was quite clear that it was not:

'*Jeux is a ballet about flirting . . . the story of this*

*Bakst costume design for
Likènion in* Daphnis and Chloë

The Chosen Maiden costume for The Rite of Spring, *designed by Roerich, 1913*

Pastel drawing by Valentine Gross of The Rite of Spring

Ballets Russes

Pastel drawing by Valentine Gross of The Rite of Spring

ballet is about three young men making love to each other . . . Jeux is the life of which Diaghilev dreamed. He wanted to have two boys as lovers . . . Diaghilev wanted to make love to two boys at the same time, and wanted these boys to make love to him. In the ballet, the two girls represent the two boys and the young man is Diaghilev. I changed the characters, as love between three men could not be represented on the stage. I wanted people to feel as disgusted with the idea of evil love as I did. . . .'

This, however, seems highly unlikely – if Diaghilev had entertained ideas of the kind Nijinsky mentioned he did not need to go to the trouble and expense of staging a ballet to give them symbolic reality. There were plenty of people in Paris like Albert Le Cuziat (Proust's Jupien) only too willing to arrange such diversions. Nor is it likely that Diaghilev would have wished his private fantasies (if such they were) played out, however symbolically, to an audience of 2,000 at the Théâtre des Champs-Elysées.

The ballet was a mess, was recognized as such, and soon vanished. The one person who had real cause to be aggrieved was Debussy. Apart from *Pelléas et Mélisande*, he never had much luck with his stage works. It was his own fault in the case of *Khamma* and the terribly weak *La Boîte à joujoux*, neither of which mattered very much. But *L'Après-midi d'un faune* had been mangled by Nijinsky; *Le Martyre de Saint-Sébastien* had been torpedoed by Ida Rubinstein's inadequacies, d'Annunzio's overblown text and the fulminations of the Cardinal Archbishop of Paris; and now *Jeux*, one of his greatest scores, had been obliterated by the idiotic activities on stage. It took the best part of 40 years for *Jeux* to be recognized as one of his masterpieces, on a level with the magnificent orchestral *Images*.

A SAVAGE RITE

The 1913 season was a mixture of ballet and opera, and the next performances were of *Boris*, again with Chaliapine (*Khovanshchina* was given later). The next new ballet was *The Rite of Spring*, first performed on 29 May. These 'Pictures from Pagan Russia in Two Parts' had been designed by Roerich, and Pierre Monteux was to conduct the vast orchestra for which Diaghilev had specifically asked. Roerich's synopsis runs as follows:

The first set should transport us to the foot of a sacred hill, on a lush plain, where Slavonic tribes are gathered together to celebrate the Spring rites. In this scene, there is an old witch who predicts the future; a marriage by capture, round dances. Then follows the most solemn moment. The wise elder is brought from the village to imprint his sacred kiss on the new-flowering earth; and during this rite the crowd is seized with mystic terror. After this uprush of terrestrial joy, the second scene sets a celestial mystery before us. Young virgins dance in circles upon the sacred hill amid enchanted rocks, before choosing the victim they intend to honour, and who will presently dance her last dance before ancient old men clad in bear skins. Then the old men dedicate the victim to the god Yarilo.'

It is impossible not to feel that the ballet represents not only a rite which is human, however savage, but the violent Russian spring which no exile seems ever to be able to forget, the cracking of the melting ice and the explosion of the earth into flower.

These are not ideas which the audience in the Théâtre des Champs-Elysées that night would have found difficult to assimilate, but the means with which the ideas were conveyed were not so much disconcerting as positively alarming. Nijinsky's choreography may have been 'ahead of its time', or it may have been perverse and misconceived, even plain bad. It certainly seemed very strange to the audience and it had been agony for the dancers to learn. One of them, Anatole Bourman, later wrote:

'Jumps were no longer completed on toes with slightly flexed knees, but flat-footed and straight-legged in a fashion to preclude the possibility of lightness, and to convey an impression of antediluvian festivity that nearly killed us. With every leap we landed heavily enough to jar every organ in us. Our heads throbbed with pain, leaving us continually with nerves that jangled and bodies that ached.'

Even allowing for the natural hostility of a classically trained dancer obliged to turn a great deal of his hard-learned training on its head, it is clear that Nijinsky was asking a great deal of his dancers. As to the music, it was of a hitherto unparalleled violence which seemed (wrongly) to bear no relation to anything that had been composed before. As is the case with *Petrushka*, historical imagination is required to help one to try to understand how a 1913 audience must have felt when confronted with the *Rite*. Apart from the strangeness of the music, it was also probably the most brutal assault on their ears that any of them had ever experienced.

The audience was a mixture: among the usual fashionable followers of the *Ballets Russes* were members of the avant-garde. Because of the way the new theatre had been built the latter were not concentrated in the 'gods' but in close proximity to the most expensive seats. The situation was therefore potentially explosive and the explosion was not long in coming. People howled insults at each other, fist-fights broke out, applause mingled with whistling. The noise drowned the orchestra. Nijinsky stood on a chair in one of the wings, shouting numbers to the dancers. Between the two parts the house lights were turned on and the police removed some members of the audience, but with the second part it all

Caricature by Jean Cocteau of Stravinsky playing The Rite of Spring, *dated 1913*

started again with ironic calls for a doctor and a dentist as the unfortunate dancers pressed their hands to their cheeks as required by Nijinsky's choreography. Astruc, from his box, begged the audience to listen first and boo later. Diaghilev shouted a similar appeal. In the *Danse sacrale* Maria Pilz's dancing was so extraordinary that a measure of calm was restored, and the ballet came to an end. Paris had seen nothing like it since the first performance of Victor Hugo's *Hernani*, and that was 83 years ago.

There was a story that Diaghilev, Nijinsky, Stravinsky and Cocteau spent most of the night driving round the Bois de Boulogne in a cab, weeping copiously and quoting Pushkin to each other from time to time (presumably it was Diaghilev and Stravinsky who did the quoting). It appears, however, that there is no truth in this at all, and that the three Russians (without Cocteau) went quietly to a restaurant, where Diaghilev observed that what had just happened was exactly what he had wanted. This account, while less attractively romantic, has the ring of truth. The press in general was extremely hostile, but it hardly mattered. The *Ballets Russes* were more famous than ever before.

Unfortunately for Karsavina, *La Tragédie de Salomé*, to Florent Schmitt's music, with choreography by the young Romanov and sets by Sergei Sudeikine, passed almost unnoticed. The company proceeded to London, where they presented Russian opera for the first time (the two that had just been seen in Paris, plus *Ivan the Terrible*) and the three new ballets in mixed programmes. The season was a success, but there were many rows and Nijinsky insulted Diaghilev in public. The honeymoon, if such it was, was over.

CHAPTER THREE

The Struggle to Survive

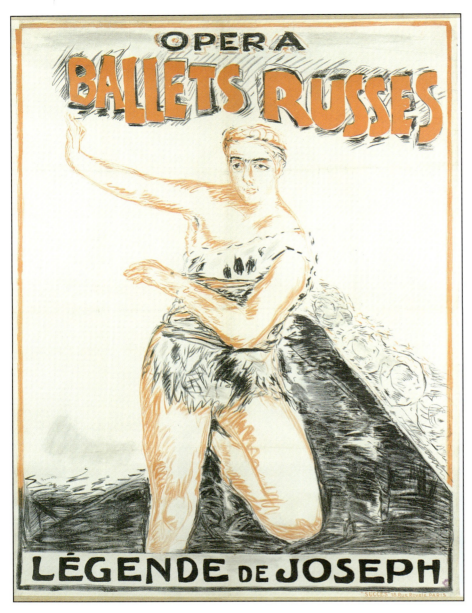

Lithograph poster by Pierre Bonnard of Leonide Massine in La Légende de Joseph, *used to advertise the first performance of the ballet at the Théâtre National de l'Opera in May 1914*

It had been arranged that after the London season the company would leave for a South American tour. Diaghilev did not go with them – he had much to do in Europe and he was afraid of the sea (a fortune-teller had predicted that he would die on the water). Romola de Pulszky did, as a trainee member of the *corps de ballet*. She worked fast, with help from Baron Dmitri de Gunsburg, who was in charge of the tour, and various others whose motives were far from being disinterested. Her engagement to Nijinsky was announced on 30 August, 1913, before the boat had even reached South America, and on 10 September they were married in Buenos Aires.

Diaghilev's reactions on hearing the news can be imagined. He had been deeply in love with Nijinsky, and perhaps still was. In any case he was violently jealous and possessive (he was extremely resentful, for instance, if Bakst or Stravinsky worked for any other company) and he had no intention of sharing Nijinsky with anyone, least of all a young Hungarian woman. Nijinsky would have to be dismissed, but not at once: he was needed as star of the South American tour. This, of course, would leave Diaghilev with no great male star and no choreographer, Fokine having resigned in rather more than a huff.

Meanwhile, the company performed in Buenos Aires, Montevideo and Rio, and sailed for Europe in November. The Nijinskys proceeded to Budapest and Nijinsky, with astonishing naïveté, sent a telegram to Diaghilev asking about the arrangements for the next season. The answer was another telegram, signed by Grigoriev, informing him that his services were no longer required.

It was quite obvious to Diaghilev that he must get Fokine back. The choreographer drove a hard bargain, but eventually agreed, provided he was allowed to dance himself, was given the title of choreographic director, and was consulted about the use of other choreographers. The Nijinsky ballets were to be dropped.

Diaghilev was now planning the 1914 seasons. Both in Paris and in London there was to be a mixture of ballet and opera. Two of the new ballets were on a modest scale. These were *Papillons*, a kind of sequel to *Carnaval*, with music once more by Schumann, choreography by Fokine, and sets and costumes by Mstislav Dobujinsky, and *Midas*, another Fokine–Dobujinsky collaboration, with music by the little-known Maximilian Steinberg. But the main offerings were the new Strauss ballet, now called *La Légende de Joseph*, a new opera by Stravinsky called *Le Rossignol*, and a most elaborate double production which was Benois' idea. This was *Le Coq d'or*, the last opera Rimsky-Korsakov wrote before he died, which, though based respectably enough on Pushkin, had run into trouble in Russia because of its principal character, the idiotic King Dodon. Even the most rabid anti-royalist could not have thought that Tsar Nicholas II, weak as he was, was quite in the Dodon class, but the fact that Dodon was a king was enough for the Russian censorship. Benois' idea was to present the three-act opera as both an opera and a ballet, with a double cast of dancers and singers. The Moscow artist Natalia Gontcharova was in charge of the designs.

During visits to Russia Diaghilev signed up Pierre Vladimirov, a leading *danseur noble* from the Maryinsky. He also found his Joseph.

While in Moscow Diaghilev visited the Bolshoi several times, and was much struck by the appearance of a young man playing minor roles in *Don Quixote* and *Le Lac des Cygnes*. This was the 18-year-old Léonide Massine. Massine was no prodigy – indeed it seems likely that at this stage he was not even a very good dancer – but he had beauty and presence. Diaghilev asked him to join his company immediately. Massine who, though

Costume designs by Bakst for two Negroes in La Légende de Joseph

young, was no fool, must have known what he was letting himself in for. He accepted.

The *Ballets Russes* danced in Prague, Stuttgart, Cologne, Hamburg, Leipzig, Hanover, Breslau, Berlin and Zürich before arriving at Monte Carlo for the season, which was to begin on 16 April.

Papillons was given its first performance at Monte Carlo on 16 April, and made little impact. Nor did *Midas*, which was the last new production in the Paris season (it was first performed on 2 June). But the three other productions at the Paris Opéra were of a visual splendour that exceeded anything Diaghilev had presented before – which is not to say that they were all masterpieces. But even if the forthcoming war had not thrown all Diaghilev's plans into confusion it is very hard to see how he could have proceeded any further down that particular road: he would have had to simplify.

DECADENCE AND SPECTACLE

Strauss's contract stipulated that he would come to Paris to conduct the first performances of *La Légende de Joseph*. He created offence by remarking publicly on the sloppiness and lack of discipline of French orchestras. No doubt he was right (and times have not changed very much in that respect – the French are not individualists for nothing) but with the prevailing state of Franco-German relations his comments were not exactly tactful. The ballet opened on 17 May. The libretto was credited to Count Harry Kessler and Hugo von Hofmannsthal. Potiphar's Wife, bored with the empty luxury of her life, makes advances to Joseph, the innocent young shepherd. He repulses her; she tells her husband that the boy has attempted to make love to her; Potiphar condemns Joseph to a horrible death; but an angel appears and rescues him. Massine, in a brief white sheepskin tunic, was Joseph, Alexis Bulgakov was Potiphar, and his Wife was played by the singer Maria Kusnetzova, Bakst's mistress (Karsavina took over in London). José-Maria Sert had carried out extremely opulent sets in the style of Veronese, and Bakst created some extraordinary costumes. When *Joseph* was given in London

Charles Ricketts gave a long description of the ballet in a letter to his friend the poet Gordon Bottomley. The following passages are extracted from it:

'La Légende de Joseph was mimed and danced in an exaggeratedly sumptuous, non-realistic Renaissance setting, with Potiphar robed like a Doge and Joseph dressed – or undressed – in skins of ermine. Potiphar's Wife (who does not dance) descends a few steps and totters across the stage on Venetian clogs. Her audacious breeches and chopins were actually worn with a mask on wet days in Venice, when the streets were flooded. Bakst has for his own purposes introduced them at a feast, during which the major part of the action takes place . . .

To a very swinging, melodious piece of music . . . manifestly by the same hand as the Rosenkavalier, the curtain swings up on a double stage or court, surrounded by a second storey of twisted columns: these are gold; the table-cloth is gold also, and there are heaps of gilded apples on the table. The music . . . drifts into weird windsounds as gold dust is poured into the balances held by the Oriental slave-dealer, who then motions to his satellites . . . who usher in a set of odalisques. These . . . evolve a stomach-dance . . . till Potiphar's Wife, who is listless and motionless throughout, suddenly motions them to stop. One girl puts out her hand to her to beg, and is thrust away by a movement of sinister indifference . . . There is more gold spilt into the balances; then the music starts chiming in a typically Straussian way, and to fresh spring-like sounds a muffled form is carried in a hammock on poles across the sky, brought on to the stage, unwrapped, and you see Joseph asleep in the carpets; he is wakened, and darts about the stage . . .

Potiphar's Wife . . . from the first sight of Joseph becomes attentive . . . When he pauses, she motions to her attendant, who touches Joseph and leads him by the hand to the dais. Potiphar's Wife rises from her throne, rests both hands on his shoulders, looks into his eyes, raises his chin to look deeper; she removes a chain of pearls from her neck, places it round his, stoops to kiss his brow with shut eyes . . . The guests depart; Potiphar's Wife descends slowly and painfully from the dais, perched on her gilded clogs . . . and crosses the stage.'

In the second scene, Potiphar's Wife comes to Joseph during the night.

'Joseph is asleep on a couch. . . . The music then shudders like the wind in a prison corridor, and Potiphar's Wife . . . passes through the columns . . . She leans over Joseph . . . He awakes, she rises from the ground, unties her hair in countless monstrous strands or ropes of living gold, and with these she starts smothering him . . . until he darts from his couch and covers his head and body with his black cloak. She  *darts after him like a panther, wrestles with the cloak, writhes about his body and his naked feet, till he leaves the cloak in her hands, escaping dressed in skin tights only, with a black band across his chest, giving thereby a more startling impression of starkness than sheer nakedness itself. She then dashes at him with a dagger . . . Slaves with torches appear, attending Potiphar wrapped in a crimson and ermine cloak. The dagger is shown him, and . . . Potiphar's Wife lies to Potiphar with her smiles and her fingers, whilst her rigid body and revulsed head is twisted into an incredible half-snake, half-Lot's Wife pose which would have fascinated Burne-Jones. Potiphar touches her in compassion, whereupon she seems to strike his chest, writhes like a snake in a flame, and buries her face in Joseph's cloak, which she lifts from the ground pressed against her lips. At a gesture of Potiphar's a burning cauldron is brought on to the stage, Joseph wrapped in chains, and irons heated.*

Then the music becomes vulgar beyond belief, a light breaks upon Joseph, the chains fall off, and a golden archangel passes across the upper stage, descends, and leads Joseph off to the Savoy Hotel – I believe – to Wagnerian apotheosis music of the worst type . . . Karsavina as Potiphar's Wife was superb. A creature of gold and marble at the start, her sinister repelling of

ABOVE: *Karsavina in costume for her role as the Queen of Shemakhan in* Le Coq d'or, *1914*

LEFT: *Costume design by Natalie Gontcharova for Prince Guidon in* Le Coq d'or, *dated 1913*

the begging dancer was evil and passionless, it suggested the avoidance of something unclean. When she strangled herself with her pearl necklace, the act was spontaneous and spasmodic like a moth meeting a flame.'

This passage has been quoted at such length because it is one of the best descriptions of a narrative ballet ever written. Despite the ballet's sumptuousness and 'decadent' *fin de siècle* eroticism, it was not a great success. Strauss was a great opera composer but a poor ballet composer (his other attempt, *Schlagobers*, is even worse), and there was far too much mime and too little dance. Indeed the only real dancing was by the *corps de ballet*. Massine was given very little to do, Potiphar was a mimed role, and even Karsavina could not do much dancing

ABOVE: *Gontcharova's design for Act I of* Le Coq d'or

RIGHT: *Alexandre Benois design for the Throne Room in* Le Rossignol

in Venetian clogs, though her acting was plainly unforgettable. Because of the war the original version of *La Légende de Joseph* was seen only a very few times. There have been various attempts to revive it, mostly in Germany and Austria, including a version by John Neumeier which piles Pelion on Ossa by making Potiphar as interested in Joseph as his wife, and for the same reason. But Strauss's music remains intractable, though in fairness to the composer the Russians had asked him (via Hugo von Hofmannsthal) for 'the most unrestrained, the least dance-like music in the world'. Hofmannsthal had also spoken about music that would represent a 'leaping towards God'. Great as he was, Strauss was never much good at conveying mystical ideas, and in any case, as is clear, *Joseph* as it finally emerged was clearly about sex in various shapes and forms.

Le Coq d'or followed on 24 May, and was a huge success – Diaghilev's last for five years. Only once more in Diaghilev's life would he attempt anything

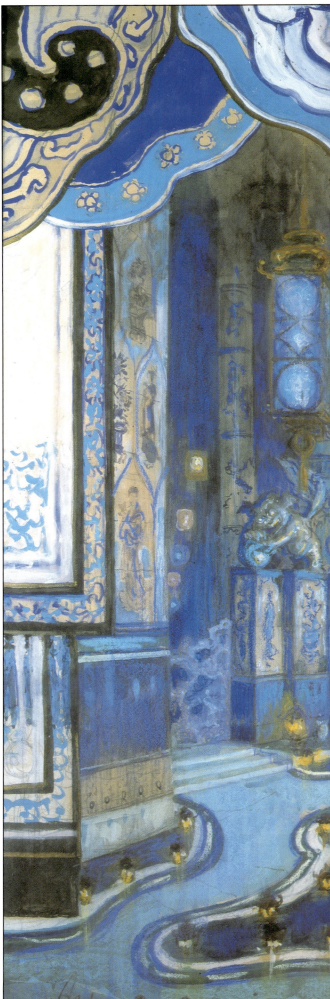

remotely on this scale, and that would end in disaster. The three-act opera tells of a feeble old king, Dodon, who consults a mysterious astrologer for help against his enemies. The astrologer gives him a golden cockerel whose crowing will warn him of danger. In return Dodon promises to grant the astrologer whatever he wishes. During a battle the King meets the beautiful Queen of Shemakhan and decides to marry her. But the astrologer asks for the Queen. The King kills the astrologer, only to have his eyes pecked out by the golden cockerel. The moral, if any, was hard to discern, but Rimsky-Korsakov's exquisite, glittering, deliberately heartless music, wonderfully orchestrated, with its exotic dances and processional marches, captivated the audiences in both Paris and London. The sophisticated 'peasant' sets and costumes by Natalie Gontcharova were carried out predominantly in yellows, oranges and reds, and between the banks of singers, robed in crimson, on either side of the stage, the story was danced out by Bulgakov as Dodon, Cecchetti as the Astrologer, and Karsavina as the Queen. When, during the wedding procession at the end, King Dodon appeared on his silver horse on wheels, Boni de Castellane, one of the leaders of Parisian taste at the time, was heard to exclaim '*C'est trop joli!*'

Benois design for the Emperor's Bedroom in Le Rossignol

Ricketts too was overcome by the beauty of the spectacle:

> '*Delighted beyond all reason . . . The music is exquisite, enchanting and original, the idea of the singers ranged on each side of the stage in oratorio fashion while the action is mimed and danced in the centre is admirable. It is a most picturesque interpretation of the principle which obtained at the birth of Greek tragedy and which still obtains in the Japanese No Dances. The interpretation was magnificent. Karsavina looked like a bewitching Hindu idol, her dancing and miming were incomparable. The intelligence of the management and the choreographic invention is also incomparable . . .*
>
> Le Coq d'or *is an astounding revelation of the highest art, admirable in realization, entrancing as music and of the utmost significance as a departure which may open a new life of art or hasten the decadence of that which exists; it is at once a return to the birth of tragedy and to its end, and quite serious people are already discussing the possibilities of its method, even in Wagnerian drama. . . .*'

The departure, alas, was not pursued (what a great many disagreeable operatic experiences one might have missed if it had been), but Diaghilev never lost his interest in presenting spectacles which combined singing and dancing. However this wonderful – and appallingly expensive – *Coq d'or* was never seen again after 1914.

In 1919 Ricketts wrote, sadly: 'Karsavina's miming of the songs was an event in my life, I shall never forget it.'

Stravinsky's new opera, *Le Rossignol*, followed a few days later. Despite many beautiful passages it is not a very strong work for the reason that it is broken-backed, the relatively simple lyricism of the first act contrasting too sharply with the exotic complications of the second, but Benois' Chinese settings were astonishingly lovely.

The London season was also a huge success. The next important performances would be at Berlin in the autumn. During the London performances Diaghilev had received a telegram from Count Harry

Kessler saying that the season might well have to be cancelled. 'The dear count must be sick,' said Diaghilev. The last performance in London was on 24 July. War broke out within a week.

TESTING TIMES FOR DIAGHILEV

During the next four years Diaghilev and his company (when he had one) led a hand-to-mouth existence. The result was that few new ballets were created, and of these few only two were of any real importance. During this unhappy period, however, Massine was trained as a choreographer, while Stravinsky and Prokofiev worked on scores that were presented as ballets after the war was over.

At the end of 1914 Diaghilev found himself with no company at all. It was not until early 1915 that the impresario, who had rented a house near Lausanne, started to try to get a company together again. From now on most of his dancers were recruited very young from ballet schools and trained under his own eye. Writing in 1930, the artist Michel Larionov recalled that at first the new company consisted of only 10 dancers, then 16, but by the end of 1915 numbers had risen to between 40 and 45. Among former members who now rejoined were Bolm, Lubov Tchernicheva, Lydia Sokolova (Hilda Munnings), and Nicolas Kremnev; among the newcomers were two Poles who were to become stars – Leon Woizikovsky and Stanislas Idzikovsky. While the dancers trained, Diaghilev was trying to

organize a tour of the United States, and badly needed Nijinsky. The dancer had been interned in Budapest as an enemy alien, and Diaghilev made frantic efforts to get him out. These eventually bore fruit, but not in time for the beginning of the American tour. This had been arranged with the sponsorship of the Metropolitan Opera House, New York, then under the Chairmanship of Otto Kahn.

Before setting off for America the newly-formed company gave a performance at Geneva under the baton of Ernest Ansermet, whom Diaghilev had hired as conductor on the recommendation of Stravinsky. This was on 20 December, and included Massine's first piece of work as a choreographer, *Le Soleil de Nuit*. This was a Russian peasant ballet to music by Rimsky-Korsakov, with designs by Larionov, and enjoyed a mild success. There was also a charity matinée at the Paris Opéra.

The company sailed from Bordeaux on New Year's Day and arrived in New York on 11 January, 1916. Needless to say, the voyage was a nightmare for the superstitious Diaghilev, who had not forgotten the fortune-teller's prediction. Lydia Lopokova joined the others in New York. The *Ballets Russes* opened at the Century Theater on 17 January with *The Firebird*, the *Blue Bird pas de deux*, *Le Soleil de Nuit* and *Schéhérazade*. The reception was good, though there was no denying that the company was lacking in fully formed stars. Doubts were expressed as to whether the behaviour of the Golden Slave in *Schéhérazade* would go down well south of the Mason-Dixon Line. The *Faune* (danced by Massine) ran into trouble too, and after a hearing before a local judge the reformed animal was reduced to sitting and looking at the famous scarf.

Taking only eight ballets with them, the dancers set off on a tour which took them to Boston, Albany, Detroit, Chicago, Cincinnati, Cleveland, Pittsburgh, Washington, Philadelphia, Milwaukee, Minneapolis and Kansas City, among other centres. The reception was by no means universally rapturous. On 3 April, the second New York season – this time at the Metropolitan Opera House itself – opened without Nijinsky, who was, however, on the way to the United States. He arrived the following day and a financial wrangle immediately broke out, with the result that Nijinsky did not dance till 12 April. *Petrushka* was a success, *Le Spectre de la Rose* much less so, the great dancer being found effeminate. All his other performances were greatly enjoyed, except for *Narcisse*, which the New York public found rather amusing.

The American visit had been sufficiently successful for Otto Kahn to ask for a further tour in the autumn, but this time Diaghilev was to remain in Europe with a nucleus of dancers including Massine,

Tchernicheva, Woizikovsky and Idzikovsky, and Nijinsky was to be in sole charge of the American operation. This decision did not augur well for the administrative side.

Diaghilev had received a personal invitation from King Alfonso XIII to bring the *Ballets Russes* to Spain. It is said that when they arrived at Cadiz from America Diaghilev was so overcome with relief that, Pope-like, he kissed the ground. Be that as it may, the company proceeded to Madrid, where they were to open on 26 May. Before the season began Diaghilev went to Paris, where Picasso was introduced to him. This historic meeting signalled the beginning of a violent – and by now much-needed – change of direction and new lease of life for Diaghilev's company.

From the artistic point of view the Spanish performances were little more than a holding opera-

LEFT: *Costume design by Benois for* Le Rossignol

ABOVE: *Costume design for the Chief Mandarin,* Le Rossignol

ABOVE: *Lubov Tchernicheva in The Good-humoured Ladies.*

Sebastian. These very reduced affairs were *Las Meniñas*, a Spanish ballet, as a compliment to the company's new host and patron, and *Kikimora*. *Las Meniñas* was a ballet for five dancers set to Fauré's well-known *Pavane*, with decor by Carlo Socrate and elaborate Velazquez-influenced costumes by Sert. Massine, who had choreographed the work, danced with Sokolova, Khokhlova and Woizikovsky. *Kikimora*, also by Massine, was a grotesque little piece about a witch and her cat, in a setting by Larionov. Idzikovsky danced the cat. Neither work amounted to much, and Massine had still to prove himself as a choreographer.

On 8 September the company set off again from Bordeaux to New York, where Nijinsky was going to meet them. He had prepared a new ballet set to the symphonic poem *Till Eulenspiegel* by Richard Strauss. The season opened on 16 October, 1916, and the one production of the *Ballets Russes* that Diaghilev never saw had its first performance on 23 October. The decor was commissioned from the American painter Robert Edmond Jones, who produced scenery that had to be lengthened at the bottom; as a result Nijinsky decided to keep this lower part in shadow. Jones described his decor (the designs for which suggest Walt Disney before his time) in breathless, semi-literate terms:

> 'A species of whimsicality run riot sets before the astonished vision a medeaeval [sic] town that never was in any age and laves it with nocturnal blue touched with shafts of crepuscular light which illuminates the inverted cornucopia roofs of tiny houses tilted at crazy angles and suggesting for all the world sheaves of sky rockets. A wonder-town in a wonderland . . .'

Nijinsky danced the part of the humorous rebel Till who is finally hanged but whose spirit lives on. The ballet enjoyed a distinct success.

The tour following the New York season took the company much further afield than had the first. They went to Texas, Oklahoma, Missouri, Iowa, Nebraska, Colorado, Utah and California; Vancouver, Seattle, Washington; Tennessee and Kentucky; then gradually back to the East Coast, where they gave their last performance on 24 February, 1917. They reached Rome, Diaghilev's temporary headquarters, at the end of March. Nijinsky stayed behind in Spain.

Diaghilev, Massine and the small group of dancers who had not gone to the United States had been in Rome since the early autumn of 1916. Three new ballets were being prepared for the spring. The first of these was *The Good-humoured Ladies*, a comedy of manners based on a play by Goldoni set to Domenico Scarlatti harpsichord sonatas, orchestra-

tion, but they were very useful in a number of ways. The King came to the opening night at the Teatro Real with most of his close family, and was so delighted that from now on he referred to himself as the 'Godfather to the ballet'. His loyalty to Diaghilev was invaluable when, two years later, the fortunes of the company were at their lowest ebb. After the Madrid performances, which were successful, the company took a much-needed holiday break before proceeding to San Sebastian, the summer residence of the Spanish Court, for a second engagement.

Two small new ballets were prepared for San

ABOVE: *Tchernicheva, Vera Nemtchinova, Leon Woizikovsky and Stanislav Idzikowsky*

ted by Vincenzo Tommasini. Massine, whose first major ballet this was, studied old choreographic manuals and 18th-century Venetian painting in order to create the effect he wanted. Bakst designed the sets.

The second ballet was *Contes russes*, an episodic ballet based on Russian folk tales (incorporating the already existing *Kikimora*) set to music by Liadov and designed by Larionov. This was a fairly uncomplicated enterprise, but the third ballet, *Parade*, was quite unlike anything the *Ballets Russes* had given before. It had sprung from an idea by Jean Cocteau, the music was to be by Erik Satie, and Picasso had agreed to take charge of the decor and costumes. Picasso and Cocteau came to Rome in February to work on the project.

There were to be some performances at the Teatro Costanzi in Rome in April. The first performance of *The Good-humoured Ladies* took place on the 12th, and was an instant success. Grigoriev wrote that 'never had any ballet given by our company been so perfectly danced, partly perhaps because no ballet had ever been so thoroughly rehearsed'. Goldoni's complicated intrigues were danced by Lopokova, Tchernicheva, Cecchetti and his wife, Massine, Idzikovsky and Woizikovsky. The movements were jerky and puppet-like, to the point that when the ballet was revived (apparently very faithfully) by Tchernicheva and Grigoriev for the Royal Ballet in 1962 there was so much frenetic jigging up and down that one was tempted to think that the choreography should have been ascribed to St Vitus rather than Massine.

After two extremely unsuccessful performances at the San Carlo in Naples, the company went to Paris for its one and only season during the war. At the *répétition générale* at the Châtelet on 11 May, 1917 *The Good-humoured Ladies* was very well received, but Diaghilev, for reasons best-known to himself, had a huge red flag brought on to the stage in the final scene of *The Firebird*. With *le tout Paris* in the theatre, Russia about to pull out of the war, and the Germans uncomfortably close to Paris, this was a foolish mistake and an error in taste.

ABOVE: *Costume design by Bakst for Felicita in* The Good-humoured Ladies, *dated 1916*

COCTEAU'S ASTONISHING PARADE

In this decidedly jumpy atmosphere *Parade* was given its first performance on 18 May. It had been long in the making. It was years ago that Diaghilev had made his famous request to Cocteau to astonish him (*'Etonne-moi'*). *Le Dieu bleu* had astonished nobody, and since those days Cocteau's style as a poet had undergone a radical change. So had his choice of artistic friends. During 1913 and 1914 Cocteau conceived the idea of a ballet that was at that stage to be called *David*. It was to make use of acrobats, a clown, and various circus characters. They were to be seen in a *parade*, a kind of trailer, for *David*, a lavish spectacle supposed to be taking place, invisible to the audience, behind a curtain. Cocteau tried to interest both Diaghilev and Stravinsky in the project, but failed. Undaunted, Cocteau continued to think about the idea, and when he grew familiar with Satie's music and met the com-

ABOVE: *Léonide Massine as The Chinese Conjuror in* Parade, *1917*

LEFT: *Picasso's design for Massine's costume as the Chinese Conjuror in* Parade. *This production marked Picasso's debut as a designer for the stage.*

Erik Satie

poser he decided that Satie would be ideal for his purpose. Much later, when Picasso too became involved, there were disagreements between the 'collaborators', and the various added noises that Cocteau had wanted (shouting, dynamos, aeroplane engines) disappeared, apart from a siren and a typewriter in the orchestra. But the final result was still startling enough to take a 1917 audience aback.

The programme note read:

'The decor represents Paris on a Sunday. Travelling theatre. Three music-hall numbers serve as a parade.
Chinese conjuror.
Little American Girl.
Acrobats.
Three managers are in charge of the publicity. In their terrible language they tell each other that the crowd takes the parade *for the interior spectacle itself and they try to make the public understand. No one understands. After the final number the managers make a supreme effort. The Chinese, the acrobats and the little girl emerge from the theatre. Seeing the failure of the managers, they make a last attempt to display their skills. But it is too late.'*

During the opening chorale the curtain rose to reveal Picasso's now famous drop-curtain, depicting circus performers at a table inside a tent, with a winged horse and its foal, a monkey, a sleeping dog and a red, white and blue ladder. There was nothing to startle the audience here – apart, perhaps, from the inherent beauty of the picture – but the decor itself, when revealed, proved to be completely Cubist, with a total and deliberate disregard of perspective. Against this the very thin 'plot' was enacted. Massine, in red, black and yellow, danced the Conjuror, Maria Shabelska the Little American Girl, Lopokova and Zverev the Acrobats. But it was the 'costumes' of the Managers which caused a sensation: Woizikovsky and Statkevitch, as the French and American Managers respectively, were encased in semi-mobile structures of Cubist 'scenery' some 9-ft tall, and could do little but gesture and stamp. The first had a property clay pipe, cane, top-hat and moustache. The second had cowboy boots and chaps, an Uncle Sam hat, a megaphone and a sandwich-board suggesting skyscrapers. The third 'Manager' was a pantomime horse with two men inside it, a charming beast with an Afro-Cubist head and an undisciplined habit of rearing. No one has ever been able to agree about Satie's music, some seeing it as cheerful and uncomplicated, others as hallucinatory, lonely and ferocious.

There was a certain amount of hostility in the theatre, but nothing remotely approaching the scale of the demonstration provoked by *The Rite of Spring*. Insults were freely exchanged afterwards, however: Satie nearly got himself sent to prison and Cocteau

ABOVE: *The original costume for the Chinese Conjuror, worn here by a model.*

and Picasso were freely described as 'Boches'. But despite the fact that the ballet acquired to some degree the reputation for bad luck which attends the 'Scottish Play' (*Macbeth*) Diaghilev performed it from time to time until 1926. It was not, in fact, a very good ballet in itself, bearing more resemblance to a Cubist manifesto. It was also the first of several works which Diaghilev was to present in which the decor overwhelmed the dancing (though the *Ballets Suédois* of the 1920s were far worse in this regard). But it gave a loud and clear indication of a change of aesthetic approach in the *Ballets Russes*.

It is interesting to note that this important ballet had a cast of only seven, or eight if you count the second occupant of the horse. It was certainly a far cry from the vast cast of *Le Coq d'or*.

A season in Madrid with Nijinsky began on 2 June. For a time there were no clashes within Diaghilev's entourage, until Romola Nijinsky once

Diaghilev commissioned Robert and Sonia Delaunay to redesign the decor and costumes for the revival of Cléopâtre *which opened in London at the Coliseum on 5 September 1918, replacing the original designs by Bakst which were destroyed by fire in South America.*
BELOW: *Robert Delaunay's set design.* **RIGHT:** *Sonia Delaunay's costume designs for Cleopatra with attendants.*

again became suspicious of Diaghilev and tried to stop her husband from going on a second South American tour which had been arranged. These disagreements were eventually patched up and the company sailed from Cadiz on 4 July. The tour was a disaster, with the Nijinskys at daggers drawn with Grigoriev and the great dancer becoming odder by the day. The *Ballets Russes* danced in Rio de Janeiro, lost a certain amount of scenery through fire in a railway tunnel, and finished in Buenos Aires, where Nijinsky appeared with them for the last time. They came back to Spain in October 1917.

Diaghilev and Massine had stayed behind, and had become friendly with the composer Manuel de Falla, already known for his opera *La Vida breve*, his dance drama *El Amor Brujo* and his 'symphonic impressions' for piano and orchestra *Nights in the Gardens of Spain*. That spring de Falla had finished a work on a libretto by Martinez Sierra based on a story by the 19th-century writer Alarcón. This was a mime drama, accompanied by a chamber orchestra, called *El corregidor y la molinera*, and it had been performed in Madrid in April. It seemed both to Diaghilev and to Massine that this could easily be turned into a 'Russian' Spanish ballet, provided de Falla could modify, expand and strengthen his score. They also found a young Spanish dancer called Felix Fernandez Garcia, who was taken on to give Massine lessons in the dances of his country. Poor Felix was to become one of the saddest characters to be crushed under the chariot wheels of the *Ballets Russes*.

Diaghilev was now at his wits end. He tried to arrange a London season with Beecham, but failed. The company danced in Barcelona, Madrid and Lisbon, but at the beginning of 1918 they had nothing before them at all. In addition, they were utterly down and out financially.

Finally Diaghilev managed to arrange a general tour of Spain, small towns as well as large. This did not produce very much money, and the dancers, exhausted and penurious, ended up at Barcelona again. Diaghilev felt that he could no longer ask

Delaunay's designs for three dancers

them to stay with him, though even now some did. The compassionate Misia Sert urged him to give up this seemingly endless and unprofitable struggle.

He did not. With the help of the King of Spain and various Spanish, French and British diplomats, it was arranged that the company and all its sets, costumes and baggage should be transported to London for a season that Oswald Stoll had agreed to give at the Coliseum.

It is impossible to resist quoting what Lydia Sokolova later wrote about the behaviour at this time of a man so often depicted, not unjustly, as ruthless, despotic, jealous, possessive, arrogant and misogynistic. It must be explained that Sokolova had borne a child (the father was Kremnev) shortly after her return from the United States.

'We used to meet him at ten o'clock at night in the park where the cafés were, and I came to love him dearly as a person during that anxious time. He often used to carry the baby himself and let her play with his monocle. One day Natasha was so ill I thought her last hour had come. Diaghilev took me to his bedroom, opened a wardrobe trunk and brought out a little bag. He undid the string and emptied on the bed a heap of copper and silver coins from various countries. This, I suppose, was all the money he had left. He picked out all the silver coins and gave them to me, telling me to get a doctor.'

He arrived in London that August and took up residence at the Savoy Hotel. The Coliseum at this time gave two shows a day, and it was arranged that the company would dance one ballet in the afternoon and one in the evening. Each would therefore form part of a music-hall performance. Diaghilev did not care for this arrangement, but he was in no position to pick and choose. He hired some English dancers to take the place of those who had left him in Barcelona. Among them was Vera Clark, who eventually became Vera Savina for stage purposes. This was one recruitment that Diaghilev would in time bitterly regret. Rehearsals began.

The season opened on 5 September, with *Cléopâtre* in the afternoon and *The Good-humoured Ladies* in the evening. There were full and enthusi-

astic houses, despite the fact that there was no Karsavina and no Nijinsky any more. But the audience took at once to Lopokova, Woizikovsky, Idzikovsky and the rest, and, most importantly, Massine's ballet appealed to the London public.

The original Bakst sets for *Cléopâtre* had been destroyed by fire in South America, and so there were new designs by Robert Delaunay. Ricketts did not like them at all – indeed he did not care for the whole thing – and his disillusioned account makes an interesting if rather sad comparison with Cocteau's ecstatic account quoted on page 28:

'Cléopâtra was a tragic medley. The hideous setting is by the post-impressionist round the corner, pink and purple columns, a pea-green Hathor cow, and a yellow Pyramid with a green shadow and red spot; curiously enough, like many efforts at intensive colour, the effect is not coloured. A few of the old dresses, grown grey and tired, stood out amongst new ones, evidently done by the same firm, I imagine, which dressed the Swinburne Ballet. These were eked out with dresses from Le Dieu bleu, Thamar, *even* Joseph, *worn by very British supers with expressions on their faces signifying "If you think I like these clothes you are blooming well mistaken". Massine dances well, but he is uninspired; he has huge square legs. . . . He is stark naked save for some rather nice bathing-drawers, with a huge black spot on his belly. Two or three idiot girls in the gallery shrieked with laughter when he came on. They shrieked again when the nice coral-red men came on, they again shrieked when Cléopâtra was brought out of her veils and when the fauns appeared.*
Will the masses turn Bolshevist or suffer in silence this intrusion of art into their national Shrine? Will the snobs, like myself, pip it?'

Ricketts could not have been expected to know what the *Ballets Russes* had been through in the past three years: it is little short of amazing that the company could manage to present any sort of show at all. Nor were his fears justified: the 'masses' loved the spectacle and the 'snobs', so far from 'pipping it', came flocking back. The season ran till the end of March 1919, almost seven months, far longer than had been planned. Progressively the old favourites were brought back into the repertoire – *Carnaval, Igor, Schéhérazade, Les Sylphides, Thamar* – while *Le Soleil de Nuit* and *Contes Russes* were introduced. Diaghilev started to build up contacts with the intellectual world of London, just as he had in Paris. These new acquaintances included Osbert and Sacheverell Sitwell, who were soon allowed such privileges as access to rehearsals.

MASSINE – DANCER/CHOREOGRAPHER

The reappearance of the company had been so successful that a further season was announced for 30

FAR LEFT: *Pencil drawing of André Derain who designed the decor and costumes for* La Boutique fantasque *by Picasso, London 1919*

ABOVE: *Karsavina and Massine as the Can-Can dancers in* La Boutique fantasque

LEFT: *Lubov Tchernicheva as the Queen of Clubs and Mikhail Fedorov as The King of Hearts*

April. This was to be at the Alhambra Theatre, and would consist of full ballet programmes of the kind to which Londoners had been accustomed before the war. Massine was preparing two new ballets, and to Diaghilev's joy they became two of the greatest triumphs he ever achieved. They also finally confirmed Massine's brilliance and versatility as a choreographer.

One of these was the new Spanish ballet; the other was *La Boutique fantasque*. This had been in Massine's mind for some time. The composer Respighi had drawn Diaghilev's attention to a series of short works by Rossini, described by their creator as the sins of his old age (*Péchés de ma vieillesse*), written purely for his own amusement and that of his friends during his long retirement from the operatic stage. No doubt prompted by earlier ballets like *Coppélia* and *Die Puppenfee*, Massine had the idea of a ballet set in a toy shop, with a great variety of dancing dolls. Respighi agreed to orchestrate the pieces chosen for the ballet, and this was likely to be a considerable asset, since he was a pupil of Rimsky-Korsakov and famous for the brilliance of his orchestral writing.

The setting of the ballet is a toy shop overlooking a bay with a paddle-steamer crossing it; it could be a Mediterranean harbour such as Nice or Villefranche, or even a stretch of water on one of the Italian or Swiss lakes. The period is the 1860s, though some of the dance movements were suggested by the drawings of Toulouse-Lautrec, which date from a rather later period. Among the toys there are tarantella dancers, kings and queens from a pack of cards, a snob and a melon-hawker, two dancing poodles, a group of Cossacks, and a man and a girl Can-Can dancer, the most glamorous of all. Various customers, English, Russian and American, visit the shop, and all the toys perform for them. Finally, the Russian family buys the girl Can-Can dancer, the Americans the man. They pay and leave, saying that they will return next day to collect their purchases. During the night the dolls come to life and grieve for the Can-Can dancers, soon to be separated from each other. The couple decide to escape. Next day, when the Americans and Russians arrive, their parcels prove to be empty. Furious, they start to ransack the shop, but the toys come to life and chase them out.

The story provided excellent opportunities for both comedy and pathos, and enabled Massine to display his very remarkable gift for characterization.

Nothing could have been less like the Fokine ballets, and the choice of designer was another novelty. Bakst had very much wanted to design *La Boutique fantasque*, but Diaghilev had other ideas. 'In the theatre there are no friends,' he once remarked, and he approached André Derain. As in the case of *Parade*, he wanted the audience to see that he was now proposing to work with the great artists of the School of Paris, still, at that time, considered avant-garde. The *Ballets Russes* were going to become international, using non-Russian designers and musicians, though the choreographers would always remain Russian or Polish (partly because there *were* no other good choreographers about – they are always a very scarce commodity).

Bakst was angry and fell out with Diaghilev. Derain's drop-curtain and set were much admired, though they had some serious disadvantages owing to the artist's inexperience of stage design. The view of the backcloth was obstructed in two scenes and completely hidden in the nocturnal episode. In general, though, the stage picture, with its very sophisticated naïveté – furniture painted on the scenery, disregard of perspective, suggestions of old-fashioned toy-boxes – was admirably suited to the story.

During the Alhambra season several dancers rejoined the company. These included Vera Nemtchinova, Zverev, and above all Karsavina, whom the London audience loved so much. The principal role in the forthcoming Spanish ballet was removed from Sokolova and given to her. Another development during the season was the loss of Lopokova, who eloped amid a great deal of publicity.

Reviewing the revival of *La Boutique fantasque* by Sadler's Wells at Covent Garden in 1947, Cyril Beaumont had this to say about the original première on 5 June, 1919:

'What a first night that was and what an audience! Not only was every seat taken, but the wide promenades were packed with keen ballet-goers determined to be present, even if they had to stand. I remember, too, the eager excited looks on the faces of the spectators and the clouds of cigarette-smoke which made the auditorium quite misty. The Alhambra Theatre . . . had a cosy, intimate atmosphere unmatched by any other theatre in London, a warmth and friendliness which gave the spectator the feeling of being a member of a pleasant club. The new ballet was danced with a gaiety and sparkle as exhilarating as Rossini's melodies, and from beginning to end the dancing was punctuated with enthusiastic rounds of applause . . . Lopokova and Massine . . . really brought the house down.'

The cast was extremely strong, and included, among others, Cecchetti as the Shopkeeper, Grigoriev as the Russian Merchant, Sokolova and Woizikovsky as the Tarantella Dancers, Tchernicheva as the Queen of Clubs, Nemtchinova as the Queen of Hearts, Idzikovsky (who was quite brilliant) as the Snob, Zverev as the Cossack Chief, Vera Clark

The Little American Girl, one of Bakst's proposed costume designs for La Boutique fantasque, *dated 1917. Diaghilev however, was disappointed by Bakst's efforts on this occasion, and transferred the commission for costumes and decor to André Derain.*

The costume for André, another of Bakst's rejected designs for La Boutique fantasque

Programme cover for the Ballets Russes 1919–20 season at the Paris Opéra, showing two costume designs for Le Tricorne

and Kremnev as the Poodles, and Lopokova and Massine as the Can-Can dancers. *La boutique fantasque* was the most durable popular success the *Ballets Russes* had achieved since 1914, and the standing of the company was now completely vindicated. And a still finer ballet was shortly to follow.

During this time the unfortunate Felix Fernandez was steadily going mad. He had served his purpose and was now of little more use, since he could not keep to the same choreography from one performance to the next. Somehow or other he had formed the impression that it was he, not Massine, who was to play the lead in the Spanish ballet. He was eventually found dancing in front of the altar in St Martin's-in-the-Fields, and taken to a lunatic asylum, where he died in 1941.

The ballet to which Felix Fernandez had contributed was first danced on 22 July, 1919. This was *Le Tricorne* (*The Three-cornered Hat*). At Diaghilev's wish, de Falla had immensely strengthened his original score for *El corregidor y la molinera*. The size of the orchestra had been increased; there was now an electrifying opening, before the rise of the curtain, with a fanfare on trumpets and drums, followed by clapping, castanets, *Olés*, and the voice of a flamenco singer; the Miller, the hero of the story, had been given the now famous *farruca* as his solo; and de Falla had written a long, elaborate, triumphant *jota* for the end of the ballet. To all intents and purposes, it was a new work.

Picasso had also excelled himself, and produced what must be one of the greatest decors of all time. *Parade*, his first stage work, was more an artistic manifesto than a ballet. It was further hampered by the fact that all three of the principal contributors, Cocteau, Satie and Picasso, were trying to say something different to the public, with the result that the unfortunate choreographer never really had a chance. In the present case both composer and designer worked as hard as they could to see that the choreography could be seen to the greatest advantage, and Massine was worthy of their loyalty. Picasso's drop-curtain depicted a man, four women and a boy in a box overlooking a bull-ring, while the set itself showed an open space outside the Miller's house, baking in the heat of an Andalusian summer, with a narrow bridge beyond, and further back still the outline of two mountains overlooking a distant pueblo. The predominant colours were pink, cream, grey, white and pale blue. The costumes were in bolder colours, making much use of stripes and spots, and each one, as it appeared, seemed to add something new to the general effect. The striped costumes of the police, for instance – 'brutal-looking ruffians with blued chins and pock-marked faces', as Beaumont says – contributed

RIGHT: *Léonide Massine as The Miller in* Le Tricorne

FAR RIGHT: *Vera Nemtchinova and Léonide Massine in* Le Tricorne

positively to the movements Massine devised for their entrance. The bridge provided an upper level of which the choreographer made masterly use in the finale.

Nothing could have been a more striking demonstration of Massine's versatility than *Le Tricorne*, coming as it did on the heels of *Boutique*. Not only were the subjects utterly different; the ballets themselves were of a totally disparate kind, *Boutique* being devised for a cast composed effectively of nothing but soloists, while *Le Tricorne* had three sharply defined leading roles and important dances for the *corps de ballet*. It is probably Massine's masterpiece, if one has to pick one work from among so many, and if one is lucky enough to chance on a competent revival, much of the work's power and beauty is still apparent.

The plot is a tale of jealousy and intrigue. A miller is jealous of his wife, who is beautiful but entirely faithful to him. She has caught the eye of the local corregidor or magistrate (whose three-cornered hat gives the ballet its title), but husband and wife jointly get rid of him. However, he then sends policemen to arrest the miller and take him to jail. Profiting by the miller's absence, the corregidor renews his advances, but the miller has escaped and in the end the lecherous magistrate ends up being tossed in a blanket.

Writing in the 1930s, Caryl Brahms had this to

The Struggle to Survive

say about the ballet:

'Le Tricorne sets a little world upon the stage. The people that move about in it have been living there for a long time. When they leave the stage it is to continue their lives in the wings. These are no "balletic symbols": they differ only from people in an actual world by the brevity of their impact upon us and by the intensity of their rate of living . . . Here, too, is the perfect situation for the play of Massine's wit. The ballet has one moment of supreme poignancy, and this is when the young Miller's Wife is left alone upon the darkening stage (for the Miller has been consigned to the Corregidor's dungeons) and, in the deserted shadow of the little bridge, she flutters her hands behind her in a very ecstasy of Spanish loneliness.'

This last moment is also one of the most beautiful in the whole score.

The dancers on the first night were Massine, Karsavina and Woizikovsky in the three leading roles, with Idzikovsky in the small part of the Dandy. The success was total. Only Ernest Newman struck a sour note. In those days writers on dance as such hardly existed, with the result that ballet was regularly thrown to the wolves, in the form of the music critics. Newman was in some ways the most obtuse example of this breed that England was ever cursed with (an achievement of a kind in itself), and he was not quite sure that de Falla was at his best. Naturally, he did not like the sets. But his reaction was a curious and unimportant one amid the general chorus of praise.

The season ended eight days later, but there was to be a third one – this time at the Empire Theatre – starting on 29 September. 1919 was a wonderful year for the Diaghilev Ballet.

During the holiday, which Diaghilev and Massine spent in Italy, they had the idea of a *commedia dell'arte* ballet which would be centred on the figure of Pulcinella. The music was to be by the 18th-century Neapolitan composer Pergolesi, and Stravinsky was asked to make a suitable arrangement of the pieces Diaghilev had chosen. The composer had also prepared *Le Chant du Rossignol*, a so-called 'symphonic poem' (nothing could be less symphonic), based on his earlier opera *Le Rossignol* but without the Act I music and with no singing. Designs were commissioned from Matisse, a complete newcomer to the stage who managed, however, to produce an attractive picture. The more Diaghilev commissioned sets and costumes from French easel painters with little or no knowledge of stage design, the more heavily dependent he became on loyal and accomplished scene-painters such as Vladimir Polunin and the Georgian Prince Alexander Schervashidze, who developed a positive genius for turning vague designs into satisfactory final results.

After the last London season of the year was over, the *Ballets Russes* proceeded to Paris for the first of two seasons they were to give there in 1920. *Le Chant du Rossignol* had its first performance at the Paris Opéra on 2 February, with Karsavina as the real nightingale, Idzikovsky its mechanical rival, and Sokolova (with a necklace of skulls) as Death. The story, based on Hans Andersen, was essentially that of the original opera, but much speeded up (*Le Chant du Rossignol* is a fairly short work). The beautiful singing of the real nightingale has made it

Diaghilev with Vladimir Polunin the scene-painter (centre) and Picasso in Polunin's studio in Covent Garden, London

the favourite of the Emperor of China, but when a mechanical bird, encrusted with jewels, arrives as a present from the Emperor of Japan, the real nightingale is banished. But when the Emperor falls ill and Death appears to claim him, the real nightingale returns and saves its master. The ballet was not a great success (Balanchine was asked to try again in 1925), but Matisse's decors, predominantly white and turquoise-blue, were very striking, as were his costumes, notably Death's red tights and heavy red cloak lined with black. When the Emperor was saved, he rose in his bed and a huge red cloak unrolled dramatically from his shoulders and covered half the stage area.

After the Monte Carlo spring season the company returned to the Paris Opéra and gave the première of *Pulcinella* on 15 May, with a cast led by Karsavina, Tchernicheva, Nemtchinova, Massine, Idzikovsky, Zverev and Cecchetti. The extremely complicated plot was concerned with amorous intrigue, separated lovers, tyrannical fathers – the stock figures and situations of the *commedia*

Picasso's decor for Le Tricorne

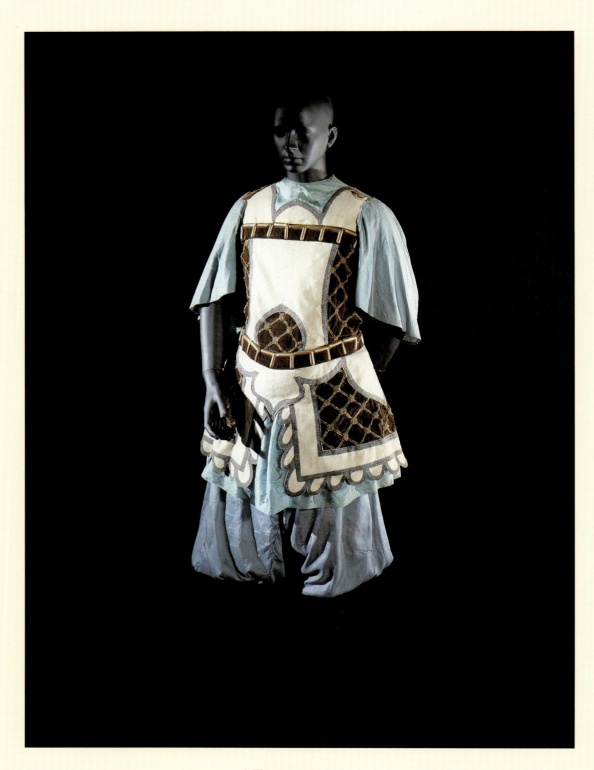

A Warrior, *one of Matisse's costume designs for* Le Chant du Rossignol. *This was a revised version of the earlier opera* Le Rossignol

The Struggle to Survive

Programme cover for the 1923 production of Pulcinella *at the Gaieté Lyrique theatre, Paris, showing Picasso's preliminary design for the decor.*

dell'arte – and all was put to rights at the end through the influence of Pulcinella. Picasso's decor showed a perspective of houses by the sea, Cubist in style and wonderfully atmospheric, carried out principally in blue, white, grey, brown and black. This had not been Picasso's original idea: his earlier designs were for a theatre within a theatre, either Neapolitan or Parisian, but Diaghilev had rejected them and there had been an angry scene, with either the Russian or the Spaniard (accounts differ) throwing Picasso's work on the floor and stamping on it furiously.

Where the music was concerned, Diaghilev got both less and more than he bargained for. He had told Massine that the music would be scored for what he called, rather quaintly, 'a large orchestra with harps'. What emerged was a ballet with songs in one act and eight scenes scored for soprano, tenor and bass soloists, and a chamber orchestra. The impact of this work resounded through the following decade, for Stravinsky had not been content with tactful arrangements of the kind practised by Respighi in *Boutique* or Tommasini in *The Good-humoured Ladies*: he had completely recomposed the music, producing a result that was quite as much Stravinsky as Pergolesi, indeed rather more so. It was violently attacked by certain musicians, but to listeners today the 18th-century crispness of Pergolesi and the 20th-century crispness of Stravinsky sit well together. While it is not true to say that other composers rushed to perform similar operations on 18th-century originals, *Pulcinella* spearheaded what was to be known as the neoclassic movement in music. Its spareness of outline, modesty of aim, and emphasis on tunes led to a kind of return to the elegant hedonism of 200 years before. The finale of Poulenc's *Les Biches*, for instance, is a very close relative of the last pages of *Pulcinella*. How many scores first produced *nowadays* in the ballet theatre have an immediate effect on what other composers are doing? The Diaghilev Ballet was unique in its direct influence on the other arts and even, perhaps, some aspects of behaviour, a point which will be returned to in a consideration of the true value of the company's output in the last eight years of its existence.

Diaghilev never lost interest in presenting spectacles which combined singing and dancing, though he was never again able to embark on anything as lavish as *Le Coq d'or*. Later on he tried to interest the Monte Carlo audience in his opera productions, but they wanted more conventional fare and he was obliged to give up. His last new production in Paris was Cimarosa's opera *Le astuzie femminili* ('The Wiles of Women'), with six singers and a final danced divertissement. The first night was on 27 May. The choreography was again by Massine and the sets and costumes were by José-Maria Sert. Coming so soon after *Pulcinella*, Sert's designs looked clumsy and dated, while Sokolova described the costumes as hideous. The danced section was soon being given on its own under the title of *Cimarosiana*. After Paris, the company moved to Covent Garden.

Stravinsky had no more new ballets to offer as yet, and so Diaghilev decided he would revive *The Rite of Spring*, but with new choreography by Massine. This would avoid the eccentricities of Nijinsky's version and bear a more straightforward relationship to peasant dances. The only problem was the vast orchestra, which would cost a great deal. At this point a new patroness appeared.

Gabrielle ('Coco') Chanel had started from extremely humble origins but was by now a very rich woman. She had become friendly with Misia Sert, and it was partly thanks to Misia that Chanel's rapid ascent in society had begun (though years later the Princesse de Polignac refused to receive her, saying that she did not entertain tradeswomen – ironic, this, in view of the fact that Winaretta de Polignac's money came from the manufacture and sale of sewing-machines; but it was she, too, at one of her musical evenings, who firmly directed Satie to the *second* supper-room, where the other artists were eating separately from her guests). Most people were less fussy about Chanel, especially in view of her power and her money.

Through the Serts she had met Diaghilev in Venice. She knew that he was in need of money for the *Rite*. One day she called at his hotel, and he had difficulty in remembering who she was. She told him that she had thought about the *Rite* and would like to help, provided the matter was never mentioned again. She then gave him 300,000 francs. It was the first step to becoming a highly useful patron and good friend to Diaghilev, and thus to the ballet in general.

The new version of *The Rite of Spring* was first shown to the public on 15 December, 1920, during the winter season at the Théâtre des Champs-Elysées. Sokolova danced the part of the Chosen Virgin, and it was her greatest role. It was also an enormous strain. Writing 16 years later (in a group of essays called *Footnotes to the Ballet*), she could still vividly recall the experience:

> *'As the moment drew near for the enormous group of about sixty people formed by the ballet to move back, leaving me alone in the centre of the stage, I could feel the cold perspiration gathering on my hands as I stood with fists clenched. The tensity of that moment was overpowering . . . With my eyes fixed on a red "Exit" light at the back of the theatre, I lived the role . . .*

The new version of The Rite of Spring *with Lydia Sokolova as the Chosen Virgin, 1920*

Those who know the music of this famous dance will remember how it works up to an absolute frenzy. This was interpreted by Massine by huge jumps round and round the stage, until at the last moment, like a deeply inhaled breath, I held myself poised on my points, before literally collapsing exhausted in the middle of the stage. The sensation following the dance was indescribable. The nearest description I can give is that my heart was bursting and that I felt I could never recover my breath again. Always Woizikovsky and Hoyer were the ones who pulled me up and stood me on my feet, and I can honestly say that I was all but unconscious until the curtain had fallen and risen three times.'

Both Massine and Stravinsky himself, who was present, were delighted with Sokolova's performance, and this time the ballet created no trouble with the audience. Trouble was indeed looming, but on this occasion it was to be on the personal rather than the artistic front.

It was in Rome that things came to a head. Massine had fallen in love, or thought he had, with Vera Savina, who was delighted and too innocent to foresee what Diaghilev's reaction would inevitably be.

The truth was that Massine wanted his independence. He was now in his mid-20s, a great dancer, and the most famous choreographer in the world. So far as is known, he never had any genuine homosexual feelings, and it could reasonably have been said (if reason ever came into such matters) that whatever he owed to Diaghilev he had now paid back, physically, emotionally and artistically. He was highly intelligent and had become sophisticated. He was also a very strong character, and his position of prolonged tutelage had grown intolerable.

Diaghilev had been suspicious for some time, but he was not sure whether it was Savina or Sokolova whom he had to fear. He resorted to the use of private detectives and there were a number of disagreeable and embarrassing scenes. Finally he instructed Grigoriev to tell Massine that he was dismissed. Diaghilev then withdrew for several days and appears to have had a total emotional collapse. He had not only lost his greatest artistic asset: he had also lost the man he passionately loved and whom he had turned from a somewhat mediocre young soloist into an international star. Truly there were no friends in the theatre.

CHAPTER FOUR

Classicism, Neoclassicism and Experiment

Classicism, Neoclassicism and Experiment

LEFT: *Souvenir programme for* The Sleeping Beauty *at the Alhambra Theatre, London in 1921*

ABOVE: *Bakst's costume design for the Queen and her pages*

Diaghilev could not hide from the world indefinitely. The season in Rome had to be completed, and there were engagements in Lyons and Madrid. Massine's roles were re-allocated, Woizikovsky taking the lion's share. This was in the short term; in the rather longer term the company was without a choreographer, a potentially disastrous situation.

Towards the end of February, 1921 an attractive 16-year-old called without an appointment on Diaghilev, who was staying at the Hôtel Continental in Paris. This was Boris Kochno, an aristocratic Ukrainian with poetic aspirations who had escaped from Russia and come to Paris via Turkey. He was taken under the wing of the painter Sergei Sudeikine and his wife Vera (who was falling in love with Stravinsky at the time and was later to marry him). Sudeikine invented a message for Kochno to deliver to Diaghilev. The stratagem worked much better than anyone could have expected: on their second meeting Diaghilev asked Kochno whether he would care to become his secretary. Naturally the answer was yes.

Kochno, however, did not become the next great love of the impresario's life. Instead, the young Ukrainian became a close and trusted friend, on whose keen intelligence and excellent taste Diaghilev relied more and more over the next eight years. Kochno became a seemingly inexhaustible source of good ideas for ballets; Diaghilev turned him into an expert on lighting; and, at the other end of the scale, he would do anything from packing the bags when there were no servants available, to tending Diaghilev lovingly when he was suffering from an illness not only fatal but repellent. The fact that he worked behind the scenes has disguised the fact that Kochno is one of the most important figures in 20th-century ballet. To give only one instance, it was he who created the *Ballets des Champs-Elysées*, the young French company which made so dazzling an impression in the late 1940s and early 1950s.

Diaghilev took Kochno to Madrid with him for the March season. There had to be some new ballets for Paris. Who was to choreograph them? Diaghilev found two temporary solutions. The first was to entrust Prokofiev's new score (*Chout*) to the dancer Taddeus Slavinsky, working under the supervision of Michel Larionov, who was to design the ballet. The second was to export lock, stock and barrel a small troupe of Spanish dancers and singers whom the Russians had found in Seville. This was the *Cuadro Flamenco*. There were also plans for a Pushkin opera with libretto by Kochno and music by Stravinsky, and for a production of *The Sleeping*

Beauty, which had never been seen in the West.

The Paris season was only for a week and was at the Gaieté-Lyrique, a theatre in an unfashionable district well to the east of the Opéra and north of the Châtelet. *Chout* was first seen on 17 May. Its subsidiary title, *How a Buffoon Fooled Seven Other Buffoons*, gives a pretty good idea of the ballet's character. It was based on a folk-tale concerned with a magic whip, and no one liked it very much. Larionov's sets and costumes, very brightly coloured, were a synthesis of Cubism and Russian peasant art. The most distinguished contribution was Prokofiev's. This was his first ballet to be produced (the first he had written, *Ala and Lolli*, had been rejected by Diaghilev as being too reminiscent of the *Rite*), but he was to write two more for the *Ballets Russes*, and later, of course, *Romeo and Juliet*, *Cinderella* and *The Stone Flower* for Soviet companies.

Cuadro Flamenco was given its first Paris performance on the same night as *Chout*.

When the company proceeded to London at the end of May they appeared for the first time at the Prince's Theatre, which belonged to the impresario C. B. Cochran, and the stage was really too small for a company like Diaghilev's. It was a 10-week season. *Chout* was not very popular, many feeling, probably quite correctly, that what dancing there was had been swamped (as it had been in *Parade*). Cochran says that one critic felt that *Chout* could well be 'frightfully entertaining to bloodthirsty children and homicidal lunatics'. *Cuadro Flamenco*, however, caught the fancy of the public. Some of it sounds rather on the gruesome side – there was a female dwarf and, worse still, a legless man who danced the *zapateado* on his stumps – but London stomachs were evidently stronger than one might have expected, and the only person who objected was the Spanish Ambassador. Picasso had designed a pretty set with four stage boxes. The King of Spain came to see the *Cuadro* and liked it very much. Together with *Le Tricorne*, it created a wide interest in Spanish dancing in general.

The season ended on 30 July. About this time Diaghilev agreed with Oswald Stoll that *The Sleeping Beauty* would be presented at the Alhambra Theatre towards the end of the year for a run of performances, and Stoll and his board made £10,000 available for the sets and costumes. Diaghilev had embarked on one of his greatest adventures.

He was taking an enormous risk, as he must have known. Neither London nor Paris had taken greatly to *Giselle* or *Le Lac des Cygnes*. He had accustomed audiences to barbarously sophisticated (or sophisticatedly barbarous) spectacles such as *Igor*, *Schéhérazade* and *Thamar*, and to witty character ballets such as *La Boutique fantasque* and *Le Tricorne*. Would they accept the pure, unadulterated classicism of Petipa? Nowadays, of course, the great 19th-century ballets provide the safest way to fill a house (especially if danced, in however mediocre a manner, by Soviet Russians), but this was by no means the case in the early 1920s. Diaghilev and his early collaborators, like Bakst and Benois, had never rejected the great tradition: they had merely objected to certain aspects of it which had degenerated into routine – for instance, the quality of the designs, which, though lavish, lacked taste and imagination, the inferior quality of most of the music, and the inadequate use of the talents of the male dancers.

Confident in the quality of what he was about to present, Diaghilev set out to out-Maryinsky the Maryinsky. He had wanted Benois, that expert in the 17th and 18th centuries, to design the ballet, but Benois was working in Leningrad and would not leave without guarantees which his old friend could not accept. Diaghilev therefore turned to Bakst, whose last major commission this was. His decision was providential, since while Benois had talent Bakst was a genius, and on this particular occasion he excelled himself.

It was essential to introduce new blood into the company for the task ahead. If the ballet were to be played night after night for a series of performances, not one but several Auroras were needed. Karsavina would have been the ideal choice as one of them, but she was not available. Diaghilev signed up Lubov Egorova, late of the Maryinsky, who was in Paris; then Olga Spessivtseva (Spessiva), another Maryinsky ballerina who was currently living in poverty in Riga; Vera Trefilova, who was 46 and had not danced in public for 10 years, and yet came to be considered by some as the greatest of Auroras; and Lopokova, who was a great soubrette rather than a ballerina, but was given the chance to dance Aurora occasionally, instead of her usual roles, the Lilac Fairy and the Princess Florine. The original Aurora, Carlotta Brianza, agreed to mime the role of the Wicked Fairy, alternating with Cecchetti.

Pierre Vladimirov, whom Diaghilev had originally taken on in 1914, at the same time as Massine, and who had now escaped from Russia, was to alternate as Prince Florimund with Anatole Vilzak, 23-years-old, a former principal with the Maryinsky who excelled as a *danseur noble*. Idzikovsky, of course, would dance the Blue Bird. Nijinsky's sister Bronislava, who had acquired experience as a choreographer in Russia, was hired, her first task being to invent additional dances for the ballet. Nicolas Sergeyev, a former Maryinsky ballet-master, was in Paris also: he was capable of reconstructing the original production from his notes. Stravinsky,

Bakst's costume design for the King's Negro, The Sleeping Beauty

a passionate admirer of Tchaikovsky, advised on modifications to the score, the insertion of additional numbers taken from *The Nutcracker*, and matters of orchestration. Eugene Goossens, whose concert performances of *The Rite of Spring* had done so much to win audiences over to the work, was to conduct, alternating with Gregor Fitelberg, the Polish musician who was a friend of Szymanowski and fellow-member with him of the 'Young Poland' group. Bakst was hard at work in Paris, studying 17th- and 18th-century designs such as those of the Bibienas in a search for ideas for the immense production that had been undertaken.

Bakst's costume design for a Duchess. The Sleeping Beauty

A BLIGHTED DREAM

The cost escalated to the point where only a very long run of performances could possibly cover it. It remained to be seen whether this would be possible. The opening night was 3 November, 1921, when the curtain rose on one of the most splendid spectacles London had ever seen. Despite all the rehearsals, however, there were two technical failures: the forest which grows up around the Palace at the behest of the Lilac Fairy got stuck, and the gauze curtains which were intended to add mystery to the Prince's journey by boat in search of the Princess (the so-called *Panorama*) piled up on top of one another like a bale of muslin. These mistakes could be rectified at subsequent performances, but Diaghilev had already decided that his enterprise was blighted. That night, at the Savoy, he broke down from disappointment and exhaustion.

He was right. The enterprise *was* blighted. Incredible as it may seem, Tchaikovsky's seemingly inexhaustible flow of melodic invention passed almost unnoticed. So did Petipa's choreography, which, with the *Grand pas des fées, Rose Adagio, Blue Bird pas de deux,* and *Grand pas de deux*, now seems one of the towering heights of balletic invention. Praise was in general reserved for Bakst and for individual dancers, notably Lopokova and Idzikovsky. Ernest Newman spoke with relish in the *Sunday Times* of the suicide of the *Ballets Russes*. Lest one should think that the entire London ballet public was afflicted with temporary madness, it is instructive to read what Anton Dolin, who, as Patrikief, appeared in the production at the age of 17, had to say in 1939, in an article attacking Arnold Haskell for praising the new Sadler's Wells production at the expense of Diaghilev's:

> 'No words of mine could ever hope to convey even a faint impression of that monument of massed superlatives which was Serge Diaghilev's 1921 production of The Sleeping Princess, *but I had the honour to be in it – as a member of the* corps de ballet *– and I know that it was, without any shadow of doubt, the most stupendous ballet production that London has ever seen. I was only a schoolboy at the time and was particularly thrilled by the growing forest: softly and majestically it rose through the earth, mass after mass of it, slowly and insidiously it crept towards the castle in which the Princess Aurora had just fallen into her century-long sleep.*
>
> The Sleeping Princess *was truly a gigantic production, everything about it was to scale, even its failure, which was colossal. And why did it fail? Well, 17 years ago Miss Ninette de Valois had not yet done her "yeoman" service for the dance and the London public had never before been asked to sit through a ballet – and that a purely classic one – which lasted the whole evening. They wanted a few character dances. They were used to quite a lot of jam with their powder and, being the English public, they liked what they were accustomed to. They did not want all that unadulterated classicism and, to their undying shame, they left Serge Diaghilev's mightiest production to play to an empty theatre. Now, thanks to Sadler's Wells, the London public has been broken in to full-length ballet, and loves it. But in 1921–22 three ballets a night were the usual thing and anything else was regarded as an unwelcome innovation.'* (It should be explained that Diaghilev had renamed the ballet because he thought that for an English audience the title *The Sleeping Beauty* would suggest pantomime.)

There were some in London who fell in love with the production and came back again and again to see their favourite dancers and compare performances. This was a new phenomenon in the West, though it had been common enough in Russia. Spessiva, who had danced the first Aurora, had her 'fans', as had Trefilova. On one occasion Trefilova held a balance far longer than anyone could have thought possible. Spessiva remarked that she was simply balancing against the thigh of her cavalier, Vladimirov. Trefilova did not take this well. Dolin tells the story of what happened at her next performance:

> *'When the moment came for the celebrated* arabesque, *Vladimirov, who had been warned beforehand, moved away to the other side of the stage, leaving Trefilova standing perfectly and most wonderfully poised on one point in a supreme* arabesque *position for as long as she wanted, and for that one occasion with a complete disregard for the music. The audience went wild . . .'*

While this anecdote of Trefilova's behaviour makes her sound, for those of us who remember Toumanova, like the latter at her worst, it was a highly effective way of answering her rival.

But despite a visit by the King and Queen, audiences continued to diminish, while bills continued

Bakst's costume design for a negro servant, The Sleeping Beauty

RIGHT: *Bakst's costume design for a Minister of State,* The Sleeping Beauty

to arrive. The season closed on 4 February after 105 performances, and Oswald Stoll confiscated the sets and costumes. The great production was never seen again.

Diaghilev returned to Paris with Kochno, utterly insolvent. In his memoirs he wrote that the catastrophe had taught him a lesson: 'I realized that I was receiving an occult warning . . . that it was not my business to revive the glories of a bygone age.'

Nor did he again, and at this point it is worth considering what he did instead, for the output of the Diaghilev Ballet over the next eight years (from 1922 to 1929) has attracted a great deal of hostile and even spiteful comment.

DIAGHILEV AND THE CRITICS

Most critics writing in the 1930s – especially in Britain – took the view that the 'Silver Age' of the Diaghilev Ballet was greatly inferior to its glorious period before the outbreak of the 1914–18 War. It was not a question of differences in kind: it was a case of simple decline. Here is Arnold Haskell:

'Undoubtedly during his [Diaghilev's] last phase the importance of the dancer was at its lowest ebb; the dancer was only too often used as a marionette to express the latest craze of the latest painter or musician, cramped by costume, cramped by decor, cramped by music . . .'

And Caryl Brahms:

*'Here was a failure (*The Sleeping Beauty*) no impresario could afford. The times were out of joint with the spacious – they were attuned only to the episodic, the brief and the modish. For once Diaghilev's flair for the psychological moment had deserted him . . . He established his organization at Monte Carlo and, in accordance with his policy of uniting the young experimenters in the arts that go to make the ballet, he surrounded himself with young Latins . . . And since wit is the very coin of satire, and the Latin temperament turns to wit as the German to philosophy and the British to the open air, the Russian ballet began to laugh at its own effects with a superimposed Latin levity that destroyed for a time its great Slavonic gift of taking itself seriously . . . The* Ballet Russe *now concerned itself mainly with the* chic *and the* épatant *. . . Fashionable leaders of the intelligentsia were enlisted . . . Jean Cocteau, Matisse, Picasso, Auric, Satie . . .'*

One doubts whether anyone ever took Haskell very seriously, but Caryl Brahms demands a little more attention. Disregarding her evident command of breathless cliché, let us examine her facts. Diaghilev had not waited till after the commercial failure of *The Sleeping Beauty* to enlist 'fashionable leaders of the intelligentsia'. He had done that from the start. As to the ones she mentions, Cocteau had first worked for Diaghilev in 1911–12, Matisse in 1919–20, Picasso in 1917, Satie in the same year, and even Auric had been approached for a ballet in the spring of 1921. And who *were* all these witty young Latins? If one studies the list of Diaghilev's collaborators between 1922 and 1929 one does indeed find Juan Gris, Poulenc, Marie Laurencin, Auric, Milhaud, Cocteau, Pedro Pruna, Vittorio

Classicism, Neoclassicism and Experiment

Rieti, Joan Miró, Derain, Henri Sauguet, and Picasso; one also finds Stravinsky, Larionov, Gontcharova, Dukelsky, Max Ernst, Naum Gabo, Anton Pevsner, Prokofiev, Yakulov, Nicolas Nabokov, and Pavel Tchelitchev. And surely not even Caryl Brahms would describe Braque, Utrillo and Di Chirico, still less Rouault, as witty young Latins?

Writing a little earlier, Constant Lambert, evidently still smarting from his brush with Diaghilev in 1926, which will be described on a later page, made a much more ferocious and dangerous attack:

'Diaghilev . . . was forced into a policy of novelty and sensationalism that gathered speed as it went. By the time the audience had just caught up with his last creation he must be ready with the cards of the next trick up his sleeve. He thus found himself in something of a dilemma after the war . . . Unless he could find a new avenue of taste for exploration he would be as dated as the older dancers whom he had ruthlessly left by the way . . . He was now part of Western Europe himself – a little déraciné and a little old . . . A lesser man than Diaghilev might have found the situation beyond him, but Diaghilev, with that genius for production that was in many ways so much more impressive than the talent of those he produced, executed a series of rapid and perplexing manoeuvres with a view to establishing a mastery over a patch of intellectual ground, which, it must be remembered, was not his by racial heredity or by right of youth.'

Lambert then accuses Diaghilev of creating a *frisson* of synthetic novelty by deliberately picking collaborators with totally disparate outlooks, sets and music together creating a 'chic chaos'. This is the notion of the so-called 'cocktail ballet'. But who were these clashing collaborators? Stravinsky and Gontcharova in *Les Noces*? Poulenc and Marie Laurencin in *Les Biches*? Auric and Pruna in *Les Matelots*? Prokofiev and Rouault in *Le Fils prodigue*? Diaghilev hardly ever abandoned the *Gesamtkunstwerk* idea, and the only 'cocktail ballets' one can find during the entire eight years are Lambert's own *Romeo and Juliet* (admittedly this was not his fault), and *La Chatte* (though even here the composer, Sauguet, liked the sets and costumes very much indeed).

Lambert also speaks scornfully of various of Diaghilev's composers as 'merely the gunmen executing the commands of their Capone, who, like all great gangsters, never touched firearms himself'. But his amusing picture of Diaghilev as Demon King will not stand up to examination.

In 1930 the painter Michel Larionov wrote:

'Many people think that the ballets created by Diaghilev before 1914 were his best. This is not at all what he thought. It was during his second period that he made most effort and deployed most energy, and it was to this period that he attached the greater importance. It was a time of creative research and effort. The public would not accept everything, but many of the ballets were crowned with great success.'

It could be objected that Larionov was biased, since it was during the 'second period' that he himself worked for Diaghilev. But Karsavina, who was there from the beginning, said in the 1920s:

'Labelling this phase of Diaghilev's productions as simply an adaptation to the fashion of the day would seem neither adequate nor fair. Besides, does not the "fashion" in a broad sense express the trend of modern thought? . . . Eccentric as some of Diaghilev's experiments might have been, they were made out of the best ingredients of art, and this to a great extent explains why he held his public in subjection.'

Diaghilev's company was unique among ballet troupes in that it was an intellectual and artistic powerhouse. It showed what was newest and most exciting in contemporary artistic thinking. It would have been curious indeed if Diaghilev had not made use of the great deal of talent that was available in France and elsewhere during the 1920s. Would his detractors have wished him to spend the 1920s laboriously trying to duplicate his early triumphs? He chose to look to the future, and in the process produced, among other works, *Les Noces*, *Les Biches*, *Les Matelots*, *The Triumph of Neptune*, *Le Pas d'acier*, *Apollon Musagète* and *Le Fils prodigue* – a masterpiece or near-masterpiece every year.

Had Diaghilev lived longer, he would almost certainly have changed direction, especially in musical matters. There is evidence of this in what we know of his plans. His early enthusiasms, notably Wagner and Tchaikovsky, meant more and more to him, the 'musiquette' of his French composers less and less. After all, an unmitigated diet of cocktail biscuits (even of the highest quality) will eventually lead to a craving for something more substantial. But he never grew weary of Stravinsky and Prokofiev, who were producing excellent scores for him right up to the end.

In 1922 the end was far away. The immediate problems were to keep the company going and repay the debt to Stoll. Diaghilev managed to arrange a short season at Monte Carlo in the spring of 1922, and relied on old favourites to attract the audience. But, as usual, there had to be novelties for Paris. This year he fielded a relatively weak batch. They were going to be a small-scale Stravinsky ballet, *Le Renard*; a miniature Stravinsky opera, *Mavra*, and the final act of *The Sleeping Beauty*, to be called *Le Mariage de la Belle au bois dormant* (subsequently, better known as *Aurora's Wedding*).

The *Ballets Russes* opened at the Paris Opéra on 18 May, and the first performances of *Le Renard*

Bakst's costume design for a page, The Sleeping Beauty

and *Aurora's Wedding* were given alongside *Carnaval* and *Prince Igor*. The company, reduced in size, could still boast among its members Idzikovsky, Vladimirov, Vilzak, Kremnev, Trefilova, Nijinska, Egorova, Schollar, Nemtchinova and Dubrovska. Nijinska was now confirmed as 'resident' choreographer.

Aurora's Wedding was danced against one of the old sets left over from *Le Pavillon d'Armide* and in costumes by various hands. The choreographic content of the last act of *The Sleeping Beauty* was given more substance with various additions, notably the *Grand pas des fées*. It pleased the Paris audience more than might have been expected.

The modest dimensions of *Le Renard, histoire burlesque chantée et jouée*, disguise its importance. The story, derived like *Chout* from Russian folklore, concerns a predatory fox who twice succeeds in luring a foolish and unsuspecting cock down from his perch, only to be set upon and strangled by the goat, the cat and the cock working together. The music is written for a solo quartet of two tenors,

Natalie Gontcharova's set design for Les Noces

baritone and bass, and a small instrumental group with a very prominent part for the cimbalom, that Hungarian instrument of the dulcimer family, which Stravinsky had first heard in a Geneva café and which reminded him of the Russian *guzla*. Musically speaking, *Le Renard* is a masterpiece, and in some ways a rather frightening one: the march which opens and closes the score has a strange feeling of inevitability and the *pribaoutki* or nonsense words that are sung towards the end are savage in their impact. It is not an easy work to stage, and the usual solution is to place the singers in the pit with the little band while dancers mime the roles of the animals. Nijinska choreographed; Larionov provided the set (a log hut and birch trees with snow on them); and Ansermet conducted. The public found the music disconcerting, but the ballet enjoyed a *succès d'estime*.

After the performance, Diaghilev and his principal dancers went to a vast supper party given at the Ritz by Violet and Sydney Schiff, rich Anglo-Jewish patrons of the arts, where the other guests included Picasso, Stravinsky, James Joyce and Proust.

Not much could be expected of *Mavra* (first given on 3 June), because it was an opera and the audience wanted dancing. Nor, truthfully, is it very good from the musical point of view. Bakst, anxious to appear up to date, had very much wanted to design it, but Diaghilev gave the work to the young Léopold Survage. This was the last of many disagreements between Bakst and Diaghilev, and they did not speak again.

The Opéra season was followed by extra performances at the Théâtre Mogador, and then Diaghilev and Kochno went to Venice. A summer and autumn tour had been hastily cobbled together, but Diaghilev left Grigoriev to take charge of this. There was an extremely important development afoot.

ESTABLISHED AT MONTE CARLO

Prince Albert of Monaco died on 14 May, 1922. Albert's only son, Louis, who succeeded him, was a bachelor, and his only child was a girl, whose mother had been an actress. It was therefore necessary to legitimize this girl, now a young woman, and she became Charlotte Grimaldi, Duchesse de Valentinois. With the death of her grandfather she became the *Princesse Héritière* (Crown Princess) of Monaco. Her husband, Comte Pierre de Polignac, was the nephew of the American Princesse de Polignac, long a patron of Diaghilev's, and he and Princess Charlotte were also fond of the arts. The Russians had already danced at Monte Carlo on a number of occasions; it was an agreeable place; and there was a good theatre, with more than adequate backstage arrangements and rehearsal facilities. Diaghilev's idea was that his company should base themselves at Monte Carlo each year from November to May, dancing in ballet seasons and providing any ballet that was needed for the operas. This would keep the company employed throughout the winter and would allow ample time for new productions to be devised and prepared. Of the remaining six months of the year two, as usual, would be holidays, and there should be no great difficulty in finding engagements for the remaining four months.

As an idea it seemed almost too good to be true, but, encouraged by Winaretta de Polignac, the young couple gave the plan their support and talked the real controllers of Monaco, the *Société des Bains de Mer* (the Board of the Casino) into agreeing. Diaghilev and his collaborators and dancers were

Classicism, Neoclassicism and Experiment

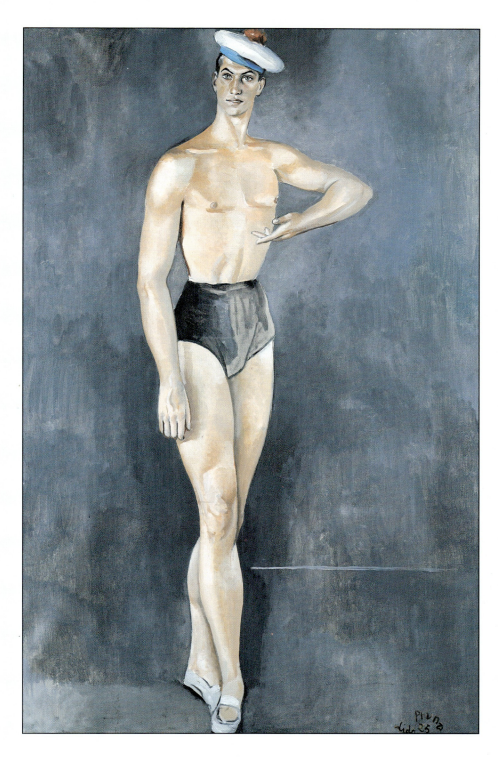

Portrait of Serge Lifar wearing his sailor's hat from Les Matelots *by Pedro Pruna, 1925*

From a series of choreographic drawings of Les Noces *by Natalie Gontcharova, 1923*

understandably overjoyed. He immediately started to make the most elaborate plans as to what he would do at Monte Carlo; many of these ideas were very ambitious, had little to do with ballet as such, and never came to fruition, but an elaborate scheme for a season of mixed French operas and ballets saw the light of day in 1924.

At this point Diaghilev reduced the number of dancers to 30 (a small company by today's standards), but he naturally remained keenly interested in any new dance talent that appeared. In January 1923 he took on five young male dancers who had been pupils of Nijinska in Kiev. None of them was particularly good, but one of them, Serge Lifar, 17-years-old and of striking appearance, immediately started doing everything he could to attract Diaghilev's attention. He was to succeed all too well. The future leading dancer Alice Nikitina was also recruited at this time.

The spring season at Monte Carlo began on 17 April. At the same time preparations went ahead for one of the most tremendous works ever presented even by Diaghilev.

Stravinsky had first thought of the idea of a ballet on the theme of a Russian village wedding in 1914, but it was nearly 10 years before the final work could be produced. This was partly because of the war, and partly because the composer experienced extreme difficulty in deciding how best the work should be scored. At an early stage he had discussed the designs with Natalie Gontcharova, and it had seemed to him then that colourful sets and costumes based on Russian peasant motifs (such as she had produced for *Le Coq d'or*) would be suitable for the new project.

Gontcharova did not begin her work until early 1916. She played with various ideas, and at one stage produced designs with which she was well pleased (and which must have been beautiful) for costumes in pastel colours embroidered with silver, pale gold, and white and grey pearls. Meanwhile, in Switzerland, Stravinsky was working on the music, and had completed the short score by 1917. He wrote that when he played some of the music to Diaghilev his friend 'wept and said it was the most beautiful and purely Russian creation of our Ballet. I think he did love *Les Noces* more than any other work of mine. That is why it is dedicated to him.'

Stravinsky contemplated various orchestral and instrumental clothings for his ideas, and he is said at one time to have thought of using an orchestra of 150 players, far larger even than the huge band required for *The Rite of Spring*. This would obviously have limited the number of performances, especially now that the lavish prewar days were over, and would probably have ruled out the presentation of the work as a ballet altogether. He experimented with pianolas and with the use of two virtuoso cim-

Svetlana Beriosova and Robert Mead in the Royal Ballet revival of Les Noces *at Covent Garden in 1966*

balom players (parts of this version still exist and they are most exciting). It was only early in 1923 that he completed his final version, which was for vocal soloists, chorus, four pianos and a great deal of percussion. Gontcharova has written that at this time Diaghilev sent for her and told her that the work was to be staged that season; the music was ready at last, and Nijinska was already rehearsing the dancers at Monte Carlo. Gontcharova says that she outlined to Diaghilev at once her simple, final ideas about the design, and he, to her astonishment, made no criticism of any kind. It must be said that Nijinska also claimed responsibility for the simplicity of the costumes worn by the dancers, but in any case they all wore uniform clothing in dark-brown and white, the girls in sarafans (Russian skirts reaching to below the knee) and the boys in shirts and breeches. The set was also of the simplest, an interior with a narrow dais at the rear, and at the back of the dais a door through which the Bride and Bridegroom would retire to consummate the marriage at the end of the ballet. Nijinska decided that, peasant ballet or not, it would be danced on point. It is said that at the first rehearsal Diaghilev was so moved that he was unable to speak.

Les Noces, scènes chorégraphiques russes avec

RIGHT: *Frederick Ashton, Bronislava Nijinska, Svetlana Beriosova and Robert Mead. The 1966 Royal Ballet revival of* Les Noces *at Covent Garden was mounted by Nijinska at Ashton's invitation.*

FAR RIGHT: *The Royal Ballet revival of* Les Noces

chant et musique (Russian dance scenes with music and song), was first seen on 13 July, 1923, during the Paris season at the Gaîeté-Lyrique Theatre. Ernest Ansermet conducted. In the end Diaghilev placed the two great double pianos (Pleyela) in the pit, which he enlarged by taking out the first row of stalls. Felia Dubrovska was the Bride, but if ever there was a *corps de ballet* work this was it, and, in Nijinska's original choreography at least, Bride and Bridegroom themselves dance very little. They must look rapt, solemn and a little frightened. In the 1966 Royal Ballet revival, Svetlana Beriosova was ideal as the Bride. The ballet was an enormous success with the Paris public, but the music critics expressed total incomprehension of the score. There were more inane comments when the ballet was seen in London, three years later. *Les Noces* was the only new production of the 1923 Paris season, but the 1924 seasons at Monte Carlo would be particularly rich, with four operas and four new ballets.

As part of his 'French Season' at Monte Carlo, Diaghilev planned to present four little-known 19th-century operas, all short. These were Gounod's *Philémon et Baucis*, *La Colombe* and *Le Médecin malgré lui*, and Chabrier's *Une Education manquée*. They were edited respectively by Georges Auric,

Classicism, Neoclassicism and Experiment

Francis Poulenc, Erik Satie and Darius Milhaud. Benois and Juan Gris designed sets. But the idea did not find much favour with the Monte Carlo public, who then, as now, wanted international opera with star singers. It is not too much of a generalization to say that the French have never greatly appreciated their own lyric theatre — where would Berlioz's works be without Sir Thomas Beecham and Sir Colin Davis, or Rameau without John Eliot Gardiner? Diaghilev took only the Chabrier to Paris, but it was the same story. His public wanted ballets and only ballets, and he abandoned any further thoughts of giving them opera, though he never lost his interest in the combination of singing and dance.

The new ballets fared far better. Diaghilev had given commissions to Poulenc, Auric and Milhaud, three members of the *Groupe des Six* whose father figure was Satie and whose 'manager of genius' (as Poulenc later put it) was Jean Cocteau. (Two of the other three, Germaine Tailleferre and Louis Durey, were minor figures, and Arthur Honegger's rather grim approach was not well suited to the ballet stage.) Later on, Auric wrote two more ballets for Diaghilev. Poulenc, unhappily, was never asked again, but the rather younger Henri Sauguet, a member not of the *Six* but of the rather similar *Ecole d'Arcueil* (Arcueil was the working-class suburb of Paris where Satie lived) was also drawn into the circle of the *Ballets Russes*. These, then, were Diaghilev's later group of French musicians, as Debussy, Ravel, Reynaldo Hahn and Florent Schmitt had been his first. One might almost include in addition the Englishman Constant Lambert and the Italian Vittorio Rieti, whose works for Diaghilev were composed in the Stravinsky-influenced style then fashionable in Paris. But, as has already been pointed out, Diaghilev did not draw all the music he needed from these sources.

Strengthened by some new recruits, the company had gathered in Paris in late August, 1923, for rehearsals, followed by a Swiss season. The new faces included two dancers who were English, or rather Irish, Edris Stannus, who called herself Ninette de Valois, and Patrick Healey-Kay, whose stage name was Anton Dolin. The importance of this event for the future of British ballet needs no emphasis. Diaghilev was somewhat embarrassed by Miss Stannus's choice of professional name — given the fact that the Valois were the French Royal Family, it was rather like calling yourself Jane Plantagenet — and he always printed her name as

ABOVE LEFT AND RIGHT: *A rehearsal of* Les Noces *on the roof of the Casino in Monte Carlo, Spring 1923*

RIGHT: *Darius Milhaud*

FAR RIGHT: *Francis Poulenc*

Devalois. Dolin was a pupil of Serafine Astafieva in London, and, as we have seen, had already taken a very small part in the great *Sleeping Beauty* (as Patrikief). Dolin was clearly going to be a virtuoso dancer. Diaghilev also fell in love with him. This was not an unhappy development: Dolin's nature was as sunny as Lifar's was sulky, and he was prepared to make himself agreeable. Like his predecessors and successors, he was presumably prepared to exploit his good fortune. Since this observation may risk sounding a shade unkind, even cynical, it is worth saying that Dolin was loyal to Diaghilev and remained so until the end of his life. But he had an independent nature and, like Lopokova in the past, he never sold his soul to Diaghilev (as Sokolova put it). For the time being, however, the company had acquired a man who was not only a *danseur noble* but also a virtuoso – the first time this had happened since Nijinsky's day.

All the new ballets had choreography by Nijinska. The season started on 3 January, 1924, with *Les Tentations de la bergère*, an evocation of a pastoral at the Court of Louis XIV with Nemtchinova, Slavinsky, Woizikovsky and Vilzak. It was neither a failure nor a hit, but Juan Gris' striking set in blue-grey and gold was so cumbersome that the work soon disappeared from the repertoire. Monteclair's music was of the justly neglected variety.

LES BICHES

A slightly muted start, then, but three days later it was a very different story. On 6 January the Monte Carlo audience saw *Les Biches* for the first time. Poulenc and Nijinska had taken to each other enormously, and the only problem during the creation of the work had been the sets and costumes. The final result was ravishing, but the indecision and vagueness of the fashionable painter Marie Laurencin – a vagueness which was particularly apparent in her watery designs – had made life extremely difficult for the scene-painter (Prince Schervashidze) and the dressmaker (Vera Sudeikina, the future Madame Stravinsky).

Les Biches was by far the most successful and the most durable of the new ballets presented that year. It was Poulenc's first work on a large scale, and his first commission of consequence. Diaghilev had asked him for an atmospheric ballet in the manner of *Les Sylphides*, in the sense that it was to be a creation of mood rather than narrative. Given this, it is with some qualification that Poulenc's own description of his argument is quoted:

'Les Biches *has no real plot, for the good reason that if it had it might have caused a scandal. In this ballet, as in certain of Watteau's pictures, there is an atmosphere of wantonness which you sense if you are corrupted but which an innocent-minded girl would not be conscious of. One such simple creature said to me: "*Les Biches *is the modern* Les Sylphides*", to which I replied, "I am so glad that is how it strikes you". This is the theme: 12 women are attracted to three men, but only one man responds, his choice falling on a young person of equivocal appearance.*

A lady no longer young, but very wealthy and elegant, relies on her money to attach to herself the two remaining young men, who seem not to repel her advances. A diversion is caused by two ladies, outwardly as innocent as doves, who appear on the scene and altogether ignore the handsome males. This

is a ballet in which you may see nothing at all or into which you may read the worst. Nijinska's rendering was inspired, for she understood its intention without really analyzing it. Diaghilev wanted a ballet in the spirit of the fêtes galantes, *and that is why he chose Marie Laurencin to do the decor; for her pictures have the same ambiguous blend of innocence and corruption.'*

Well, yes; but in this account there is a strong feeling that a butterfly is being broken on a wheel. Constant Lambert (in the course of a rather over-written onslaught on the music — one cannot but feel that he was jealous of the ballet's great success) perceptively called *Les Biches* 'Firbankian'. A synopsis of a Firbank novel such as *Valmouth* or *The Flower Beneath the Foot* would inevitably create the impression that the book was incoherent, vicious, and, worst of all, silly. Likewise in the present case to over-emphasize the 'events' which may or may not be taking place is to risk vulgarity: ambiguity is essential to the whole concept, and a stylish performance will be at pains to preserve this. Indeed if the work had not been so ambiguous the Monte Carlo and Paris audiences would not have loved it as they did. It was a quintessentially French ballet, not a German one, and to see it as a depiction of the rather disreputable activities of three homosexuals, two lesbians, a page boy, a woman with more money than sense and a number of giggling girls is to miss the point entirely. Those in the theatre were able, in a sense, to see themselves and their friends on the stage and be flattered by the comparison: such elegance might well be theirs. The ballet was not simply a reflection of a way of life (like a musical comedy or a film of the period): it was a transmutation and stylization of that way of life into a work of art. The appeal to the rich Riviera audience is an obvious one.

Poulenc composed his score for an orchestra of normal size and a small chorus of not fewer than 12 singers, the numbers to be augmented in a really large theatre. The chorus are used in only three of the numbers, the two so-called *Chansons dansées* and the group dance called *Jeu*. They sing words by Poulenc himself, a text based on French popular songs of the traditional kind and bearing no relation to the stage happenings. It soon became the practice to omit the singers entirely. This was a pity, since their voices add an interesting texture and contribute to the atmosphere, but the music can survive without them. It is a wonderful chameleon of a score, mischievous, mysterious, now sentimental, now jazzy, now Mozartian, now Stravinskian, but always quintessentially Poulenc. It is dedicated to Misia Sert, who had taken a special interest in it, especially the visual aspect of the production.

Classicism, Neoclassicism and Experiment

Svetlana Beriosova in the 1964 Royal Ballet revival of Les Biches

Pas de Trois, *the Royal Ballet revival of* Les Biches – *Svetlana Beriosova, Robert Mead and Keith Rosson*

The first thing the audience saw was the front cloth, a typically Laurencin concept with its horses, does and girls, executed in blues and greys with a little pink. This rose to reveal a room mostly white with a suggestion of a garden through the balconied window painted on the backcloth. The single piece of furniture was a vast sofa in pale sapphire blue. The *corps de ballet* were in delicately varied pinks. The 'young person of equivocal appearance' (in Poulenc's words) had sleek hair, a tight blue velvet tunic, white tights and white gloved hands which played an important part in the choreography of her famous solo. The hostess was in topaz lace, with a long cigarette holder and festoons of pearl necklaces.

The conductor at Monte Carlo was Edouard Flament; in Paris he was replaced by André Messager, the veteran conductor and composer of operetta. The three men were danced by the elegant Vilzak, Woizikovsky and Zverev; Vera Nemtchinova was the page (or *garçonne*?); the hostess was La Nijinska herself (Diaghilev was now printing Bronislava's name in this way as a well-merited tribute) – later Sokolova took over the role; and the two 'innocent girls' were Tchernicheva and Sokolova. The *corps de ballet* of 12 included Dubrovska, Nikitina and Devalois. It was that kind of cast.

The great strength of Nijinska's choreography was its inventiveness, together with the fact that it remained essentially *classical*. It is easier to see now than it can have been in the 1920s that the future of choreography lay in classicism but in a classicism which was capable of being extended, varied, distorted even, without departing in any fundamental sense from the mainstream vocabulary of the classic dance. Nijinska achieved this in *Les Biches*; Balanchine was to do so later in *Apollon Musagète* (and, in his American days, in such works as *The Four Temperaments* and *Episodes*); and it was the way forward. In this sense Nijinska and Balanchine (and indeed Ashton) represent the mainstream; Fokine and Massine (and even Tudor), brilliant as they were, do not. This is not the way things were seen in the 1930s, perhaps even much later, but it is the way they are perceived now.

Classicism, Neoclassicism and Experiment

Georgina Parkinson in the Royal Ballet revival of Les Biches *at Covent Garden, 1964*

ABOVE: *David Blair, Robert Mead and Keith Rosson with the corps de ballet in* Les Biches, *the Royal Ballet revival at Covent Garden in 1964*

RIGHT: *Lubov Tchernicheva in Massine's new 1927 version of* Les Fâcheux. FAR RIGHT: *Léonide Massine and Nicolai Efimov*

Strangely perhaps, Nijinska never approached such heights again, but a woman who can create *Les Noches* and *Les Biches* needs to do nothing else to be seen as a creator of genius. *Les Biches* was a perfect synthesis of music, dance and design – and, if properly revived, it seems as fresh and airy as it did 60 years ago.

The last of the three new ballets of the Monte Carlo season was presented on 19 January, 1924. This was *Les Fâcheux*. Kochno derived the idea from a *comédie-ballet* of the same name by Molière. The music was by Georges Auric, the set by Braque – a square surrounded by 17th-century houses, carried out in ochres and greens. The subject was a very simple one: a lover on his way to a rendezvous with his love is delayed by a succession of tiresome people (*fâcheux*) – gossips, a card-player, a dancing enthusiast, people playing battledore and shuttlecock, bowls players. The main dancers were Tchernicheva, Vilzak and Dolin. Unfortunately, the nature of the plot meant that there was a great deal of mime, and the ballet was not a great success with the public. It contained a choreographic curiosity:

Picasso's drop curtain for Le Train bleu, *1924*

ABOVE: *Anton Dolin and Lydia Sokolova in* Le Train bleu

at one stage of the action Dolin danced on point.

A season of 12 performances at the Théâtre des Champs-Elysées in Paris opened on 26 May. *Les Biches* was very much liked, *Les Fâcheux* was not, as had been the case at Monte Carlo. One further new ballet was given, *Le Train bleu*, which was intended to provide a starring role for Dolin. Jean Cocteau had seen the young dancer doing acrobatics and conceived the idea of a beach ballet which would mirror the current passion for sport and athletics. Diaghilev went in search of music to Darius Milhaud, who was then engaged in composing another ballet, called *Salade*, for the *Soirées de Paris*. For some time in the 1920s the Diaghilev Ballet encountered competition not only from the *Ballets Suédois* but also from Count Etienne de Beaumont, who was rich, cultivated and one of the leaders of fashionable Paris society. Beaumont began by commissioning private entertainments for the parties which he gave at his *hôtel particulier* in Paris. These acquired so distinguished an artistic reputation that he was persuaded to transfer them to a theatre and open them to the public. The result was the *Soirées de Paris* of 1924 and 1925. A number of artists who had worked for the *Ballets Russes* contributed to Beaumont's seasons, and Diaghilev deeply resented this. But the commercial and artistic threat was more apparent than real: neither Beaumont nor Rolf de Maré (who financed the *Ballets Suédois*) had Diaghilev's flair, persistence and professionalism.

Diaghilev tried to talk Milhaud out of working for Beaumont at all, but the composer replied that he intended to fulfil his contract. However, he had no objection to writing a ballet for Diaghilev as well. The impresario had to settle for this. Not liking Milhaud's more dissonant manner, he asked for something light, frivolous and in the style of Offenbach. Cocteau in turn wanted music 'of the kind you hear in the cinema when Mme Millerand visits a hospital' (Mme Millerand was the wife of the French President). Milhaud obliged and, having written *Salade* between 5 and 20 February, he composed *Le Train bleu* between 15 February and 5 March. He presented Diaghilev with a tuneful, jolly score which was exactly right for what Cocteau and Nijinska had in mind.

The new ballet, which was described as an *opérette dansée de Jean Cocteau*, was first danced on 20 June. The drop-curtain, with its heavy-breasted female figures, was by Picasso (though it had originally been intended for the whole season, it came later to be associated with *Le Train bleu* in particular); the decor was by the sculptor Henri Laurens; and the costumes – beach clothes and sports wear – were by Chanel. It was indulgent of Messager to agree to conduct a work which was very much a send-up of the operettas of which he himself had composed so many. The scene was an elegant beach where the train of the title had already deposited its load of pleasure-seekers, made up of a chorus of *poules* and gigolos, and the principal characters – the glamorous *Beau Gosse*, his girlfriend Perlouse, the male golfer, and the woman tennis champion, danced respectively by Dolin, Sokolova, Woizikovsky and Nijinska. There was a plot – of sorts – but

ABOVE LEFT: *Scene from* Le Train bleu

ABOVE: *Lydia Sokolova, Anton Dolin, Jean Cocteau, Leon Woizikovsky and Bronislava Nijinska on the first night of* Le Train bleu

ABOVE: *Lydia Sokolova, Anton Dolin, Bronislava Nijinska and Leon Woizikovsky* in Le Train bleu

RIGHT: *A company class conducted by Enrico and Madame Cecchetti in Monte Carlo, 1925. The 14-year-old Alice Marks (Alicia Markova) is third from the left at the barre.*

an extremely lightweight one, not for a moment to be taken seriously. It concerned the kind of happenings which occur less often on the beaches of real resorts than on the *plages* of countless musical comedies. People flirt, bathe, argue, lie about, take photographs of each other. It was all very cheerful and agreeably silly.

It was very much Dolin's ballet, and, as Diaghilev had intended, it made him a star. His acrobatics astonished and delighted the audience, and when, a little later, he left the company, no one capable of dancing the role could be found and *Le Train bleu* was dropped for ever. It could not have been more different from Diaghilev's other 'sporting' ballet, *Jeux*, and it caught the mood of the time to absolute perfection.

There was a German tour in the autumn, and a London season, the first for nearly three years, opened at the Coliseum on 24 November. Once again the company were appearing in music-hall programmes – one ballet in the afternoon and one in the evening – but Stoll could now be paid off. It was at this time that Diaghilev took on four Soviet dancers who had also been touring Germany. These were Alexandra Danilova, Nicolai Efimov, Tamara Gevergeva (later known simply as Tamara Geva) – and George Balantchivadze, a young Georgian who, as Balanchine, became the great choreographer whose work is now known all over the world.

The London season lasted seven weeks and ended with a great demonstration of enthusiasm by the public. But Diaghilev was once again without an experienced choreographer, for Nijinska had decided to leave. He decided to try Balanchine out, and invited Massine back to arrange two ballets in 1925. Massine accepted.

It was during the weeks in London that Diaghilev learned of the death of Bakst. The great designer died in Paris on 28 December, 1924. There had been no reconciliation between the two men, who had shared such triumphs in the years gone by.

During the late winter and spring the company was at Monte Carlo as usual, rehearsing and preparing new ballets. With them was the 14-year-old English girl Alicia Marks (Markova), who had been recruited in London at Astafieva's studio.

The first new ballet of 1925, *Zéphire et Flore*, was a disappointment. Kochno had devised it as an entertainment on a mythological theme to be danced as it might have been by serfs in the private theatre of a Russian nobleman. The music was by the young Russian composer Vladimir Dukelsky, the sets and costumes again by Braque. The leading parts of Zephyr, Flora and Boreas were given to Nikitina, Dolin and Lifar. The latter had by now succeeded in his determined efforts to win Diaghilev's attention and affection, and was being groomed to become a leading dancer, despite the limitations of his technique. The three ingredients in the work had been intended to jell, but they obstinately refused to do so, and the music, it appears, was amateurish. *Zéphire et Flore* was not dropped at once, but it did not last for very long in the repertory.

After some performances in Spain, the *Ballets Russes* opened again at the Coliseum in London on 18 May. They broke off for a week to appear at the Gaîeté-Lyrique in Paris. During this time Markova appeared in Balanchine's revised version of *Le Chant du Rossignol*, and *Les Matelots* was created in Paris on 17 June. Massine was the choreographer, Auric had written the music, and the designs were by the young Spanish painter Pedro Pruna, whose work might not unkindly be described as prettified Picasso. Auric's music was much lighter in style than his score for *Les Fâcheux*, and made use of some English sea-shanties.

It was a simple story. A sailor who is about to go back to sea becomes engaged. He comes back in disguise with two shipmates to test his girl's faithfulness, but she remains steadfast and all ends happily. Nemtchinova was the girl, Sokolova her friend, and the sailors were Woizikovsky, Slavinsky and Lifar. There were no other dancers. The ballet was the first great success of the year.

Caryl Brahms wrote of it:

> 'There it is, this world of sailors and their loves, established in a Marseilles that is perfectly suggested by the Pruna decorations, backed by brothel or bar, and conditioned by plaintive little airs in the modern idiom of Auric. In spite of "amusing" treatment, both scenically (a painted disc revolves on one side of the stage to suggest a change of scene) and musically, the work is strangely moving, as for instance when the faithful Betrothed dances her loneliness and shuts her ears to the easy advising of her friend ... Lydia Sokolova, great artist, magnificent mime ... danced the role of Confidante in this ballet when Diaghilev first presented it, and the memory of her conception of the role – a slow-witted, staring slyness – adds interpretatively to the choreographer's design. And when Danilova, wittiest artist of the modern regime, dances the Faithful Maid, bringing a sense of tears to the pas seul in which, shawl around head, she mourns her absent love, the ballet for just that space is miraculously balanced on a tear-drop.'

RIGHT: *Anton Dolin and Serge Lifar rehearsing* Zéphire et Flore

BELOW: *Alicia Markova in Georges Balanchine's revised version of* Le Chant du Rossignol, *1925*

FAR RIGHT: *Vera Nemtchinova in* Les Matelots, *c1925*

Diaghilev and Dolin had not been getting on well together, and on the last night of the Paris season the dancer appeared in *Le Train bleu* for the last time and left the company, to Diaghilev's great regret. Dolin knew that he was now in a position to earn a great deal more money elsewhere, but he came back to the *Ballets Russes* again before the end. Despite their disagreements, Diaghilev and Dolin always retained feelings of affection and professional respect for each other.

There was another long season at the Coliseum in London from 26 October until 19 December. The first night of *Barabau* was 11 December. The young Italian-Alexandrian composer Vittorio Rieti met Diaghilev while the latter was on holiday in Venice, and was commissioned to turn one of his existing works into a choral ballet. Rieti produced a pleasant enough score, very much in the manner of the neoclassic Stravinsky. The sets and costumes were by the French painter Maurice Utrillo. Balanchine provided suitable slapstick choreography for a plot about a wily peasant feigning death in order to outwit some pillaging soldiers. The ballet pleased the audience. It was, after all, nearly Christmas.

IN SEARCH OF 'ENGLISH' THEMES

Diaghilev never ceased to regard Paris as the capital of the intellectual and artistic world, but the London public was loyal and enthusiastic and would fill the house for far longer seasons than would have been accepted in the French capital. He also had hopes of obtaining backing from Lord Rothermere, the newspaper owner. It therefore seemed prudent to commission an 'English' ballet or two.

The trouble was that Diaghilev did not much care for English art or English music. It is also true to say that there were few English composers who would have been capable of turning out the kind of music the *Ballets Russes* needed (or indeed who would have wanted to try). Consider the leading figures of the time – Vaughan Williams, Delius, Holst, Arnold Bax. It was through the world of Diaghilev's friends the Sitwells that he found, if not exactly what he wanted, something that would do. As has been mentioned, Osbert and Sacheverell Sitwell had for some time been provided with passes to rehearsals and performances, and Sacheverell had also been used to find suitable scores to be played as interludes (one of Diaghilev's favourite ideas) and to write programme notes.

In fact it was Edmund Dulac, the illustrator, a friend of Charles Ricketts, who introduced the 20-year-old Constant Lambert, still a student at the Royal College of Music, to Diaghilev. Lambert played the impresario a ballet suite called *Adam and Eve*, and Diaghilev agreed to produce it, with certain changes, but as *Romeo and Juliet*. He ex-

Classicism, Neoclassicism and Experiment

ABOVE: *Taddeus Slavinsky, Leon Woizikovsky and Serge Lifar in* Les Matelots

RIGHT: *Design for Lifar's costume as The Telegraph Boy in* La Pastorale

plained that he needed an 'English' subject! Lambert was already friendly with the Sitwells, neighbours of his in Chelsea, and it was about this time that he appeared with Edith as one of the reciters in William Walton's *Façade* at the Chenil Galleries (with Diaghilev in the audience). One ballet had now been found, but another was needed. The form the second would take did not become plain for some months.

After a financially disastrous Christmas season in Berlin the company reassembled as usual at Monte Carlo at the beginning of 1926. While three new ballets were being prepared for Paris – *Romeo and Juliet*, *La Pastorale* and *Jack in the Box* (*Barabau* would be a fourth novelty) – Diaghilev's thoughts were of replacing Nemtchinova, who now deserted the company to dance in a Cochran revue that was being choreographed by Massine. He induced Karsavina to return for a few performances; his other leading female dancers would now be Danilova, Dubrovska, Sokolova and Alice Nikitina. In both the good and the bad senses, Nikitina had the temperament of a star, but she was not physically strong; however, the London public grew to adore her, and so did Lord Rothermere, which was useful to Diaghilev, at first.

Nijinska had agreed to come back in order to choreograph *Romeo and Juliet*, and Karsavina was to dance the lead at first, opposite Lifar. Who was to design? Lambert suggested Augustus John; Sacheverell Sitwell proposed Wyndham Lewis; Diaghilev did not like either. The talented young Englishman Christopher Wood, who was very popular in Paris, for a variety of reasons, was commissioned, but in the end Diaghilev changed his mind and approached the surrealist painters, Max Ernst and Joan Miró, to paint curtains and arrange objects on the stage. The ballet would be about a *rehearsal* of *Romeo and Juliet* and would be danced in practice dress; at the end the two principals, lovers in real life as well as in the play, would elope by aeroplane.

When Lambert arrived at Monte Carlo he much admired Nijinska's choreography but strongly disliked the visual aspect of the ballet. Despite his forceful protests there was nothing he could do about this, and the work was first danced on 4 May. It was mildly successful. Lambert's score was agreeable enough, but in a matter of months he was to prove himself capable of far better things. It was a long time before he forgave Diaghilev, as has already been noted, but towards the end of his short life he wrote:

'My criticisms of Diaghilev were aimed at his later artistic policy and were in no way an attack on his genius as a producer, least of all were they meant to foreshadow the present school of ballet critics who, alas, are unacquainted with his living work.'

Romeo and Juliet was included in the opening-night programme at the Théâtre Sarah-Bernhardt in Paris on 18 May, and it caused a riot. This was directed by Louis Aragon from the gallery and André Breton from the stalls. The surrealists, motivated at that time as much by political as artistic considerations, were attacking two of their number – Ernst and Miró – who had succumbed to the blandishments of 'capitalism' in the form of the *Ballets Russes*. The subsequent publicity did no harm to the takings.

La Pastorale, a thoroughly silly ballet by Kochno, Auric, Pruna and Balanchine, followed on 29 May. It was concerned with a telegraph boy who falls in love with a star during the shooting of a film. But even this was no 'cocktail-ballet': all the elements were consistently low-grade. Lifar, Dubrovska and Danilova were the leading dancers. On 3 June *Jack in the Box* was given. This short work, consisting of three dances, had been written by Satie in 1899. He then proceeded to lose the score, and it was discovered only after his death (it had fallen behind his piano). Milhaud orchestrated it as a homage to his late master. Balanchine designed it as a vehicle to display the virtuosity of Idzikovsky, supported by Danilova, Dubrovska and Tchernicheva as Golliwogs. The set, with its cut-out cardboard clouds,

ABOVE AND RIGHT:
Dubrovska and Serge Lifar in
La Pastorale

was by Derain. Artistically, it had not been one of the company's better Paris seasons.

London, however, was delighted to welcome them at His Majesty's Theatre for the first full evenings of ballet since 1921. Apart from the ballets that had just been seen in Paris, Diaghilev presented an evening of Satie (though the English public at this time never understood what Satie had to say), *Les Noces*, liked by the public, loathed by the critics, and defended by H. G. Wells, and appearance by star dancers such as Trefilova and Karsavina. The season was a financial success.

Meanwhile the search for the second 'English' ballet had continued. Various ideas were considered – ballets suggested by the drawings of Rowlandson, ballets with music arranged from the works of John Bull, William Boyce, Thomas Roseingrave – but none of these ideas found favour with Diaghilev. Finally he commissioned a score from Lord Berners, an established composer – up to a point – who had brought some music to show him and whom he knew from the days when Berners was an Honorary Attaché at the British Embassy in Rome. Sacheverell Sitwell was set to find a suitable subject.

The solution he found was a ballet based on the Juvenile Drama of the early 19th century. He took Diaghilev to the last shops left in London at which 'penny plain and tuppence coloured' prints of characters and scenes from Victorian pantomime were produced and sold. These were Benjamin Pollock's Juvenile and Theatrical Tinsel Warehouse at Hoxton in the East End and H. J. Webb's

ABOVE: *Felia Dubrovska in La Pastorale, 1926*

LEFT: *The British writer, Sacheverell Sitwell*

Classicism, Neoclassicism and Experiment

ABOVE: *Serge Lifar in* Triumph of Neptune, *1926.*
LEFT: *Alexandra Danilova and Lifar*

ABOVE: Triumph of Neptune – Lord Berners who composed the music, with Alexandra Danilova and Serge Lifar

RIGHT: *Danilova in* Triumph of Neptune

shop at Clerkenwell. Sacheverell devised an ideal subject for a ballet that was to be presented just before Christmas that year: an 'amusing' evocation of Victoriana for a sophisticated 20th-century audience in seasonal mood.

Serious work on the new ballet started in August at Florence, while the company was on holiday. The party consisted of Diaghilev, Berners, Sitwell, Kochno, Balanchine, who was to choreograph, and Lifar, who was to dance the lead, a sailor called Tom Tug. The plot that Sitwell devised was a mixture of melodrama, fairy-tale, and science fiction. A journalist and a sailor set off on a voyage to fairyland. Shipwrecked and rescued by a goddess, they encounter a band of giant monsters and an ogres' castle. Meanwhile, in London, a dandy is courting the sailor's wife. The ogres capture the journalist and saw him in half, but the sailor manages to escape and decides to return to London. This he cannot do because a telescope on London Bridge, the only link between fairyland and real life, has been knocked out of focus. The sailor, therefore, prudently opts to stay in fairyland, and after a transformation scene Neptune appears in triumph and the sailor, now promoted to fairy prince, marries his daughter.

Once the settings and characters had been agreed, Prince Schervashidze was asked to adapt the appropriate Victorian pantomime prints as backdrops and costumes. Pruna also worked on the project. The finished sets resembled giant woodcuts in yellow, green and dark red.

Diaghilev wanted to revive *The Firebird* and if possible *The Sleeping Beauty*, and for that he reckoned he needed at least around 50 dancers (still not a great many, if one thinks of present-day companies such as the New York City Ballet or the American National Ballet Theatre). Extra artists were recruited, and rehearsals began in Paris for the London winter season, which was to be at the Lyceum Theatre, a huge house with a seating capacity of 3,000 (at the time of writing it still exists, but all attempts to use it as a much-needed London dance theatre have come to nothing).

The ballet opened in London on 13 November, and on the 25th Lopokova took the lead in *The Firebird*, which had new and spectacular settings by Natalie Gontcharova, a great improvement on the originals. Then, on 3 December, came *The Triumph of Neptune*, tactfully dedicated to Rothermere.

One can only wonder what Balanchine, the choreographer, made of the plot, since at this stage of his career he spoke nothing but Russian, and he cannot have known anything about the Victorian theatre. The dances he devised were in general classical, somewhat influenced by the poses of the characters in the old prints. There was also a flying ballet for the fairies in the *Frozen Forest* scene. Sokolova had complained about the smallness of her part (Britannia) and was awarded a solo hornpipe in front of a drop-curtain. Apart from playing a beggar, Balanchine gave himself a solo as Snowball, a Negro (when the Sitwell brothers had been boys in Scarborough there had been a black man known as Snowball who sold flowers in the street). The ballet contained no less than three hornpipes in all: Sokolova's, another in the finale, and the Apotheosis itself (rather a heavy, stately hornpipe appropriate to the solemnity of the occasion!).

All had been confusion till the last minute, and Diaghilev stayed up for two nights before the opening supervising the lighting and even helping personally in applying glitter to the scenery. But the efforts of all were abundantly rewarded: 'English Pantomime in Ten Tableaux' was received ecstatically, as well it might have been, considering that the cast included Danilova, Lifar, Sokolova, Tchernicheva, Idzikovsky, Slavinsky, Woizikovsky and Balanchine. It was also the most lavish production London ballet-goers had seen since *The Sleeping Beauty*, with frequent changes of scene and the whole company of 50 in it, many of them doubling roles. Sokolova stopped the show with her hornpipe and Danilova, as the Fairy Queen, became a star overnight. The critics loved the work too.

Classicism, Neoclassicism and Experiment

The score was certainly Berners' best ever, with its spirited dances and its cosy atmosphere of the nursery, and it is the only music he wrote that contains striking and individual melodic ideas. There is no reason why the ballet should not be revived, although, of course, the original choreography has long been forgotten. It is possible that when Balanchine created his 'British ballet', *Union Jack*, for the New York City company, memories of *The Triumph of Neptune* were in his mind; unfortunately the music was banal and the Pearly King and Queen episode suggested that Balanchine had about as much understanding of London as he had in 1926.

Massine asked to be taken back for the 1927 season and Diaghilev, somewhat grudgingly, accepted. He also engaged Olga Spessivtseva: he wished to present the most classical of ballerinas, rather against her will, in an ultramodern ballet. Massine was set to make a new version of *Les Fâcheux*, while the new ballet was reserved for Balanchine. This was *La Chatte*, with a plot devised by the mysterious Sobeka, which was in fact merely a pseudonym for Kochno. It was based on one of Aesop's Fables. A young man falls in love with a cat. Through the power of the goddess Aphrodite the animal is transmuted into human form. Alas, during the love-making of the young man and the cat-woman, a mouse appears. This is too much for the heroine, who immediately becomes a cat again and rushes off into the wings in pursuit. The young man dies.

Henri Sauguet had been asked to write the music, and he produced a charming score. Both in its lyrical moments and its more animated ones (such as the engaging *Jeux des garçons* – for the hero, like most balletic heroes, had a group of friends) it suggests Gounod more than anything more recent. However, as we have seen, Diaghilev liked Gounod.

The sets and costumes were a very different affair. They were by the brothers Naum Gabo and Anton Pevsner, Russian-Jewish artists who had left their native country in 1922 and now lived respectively in Berlin and Paris. Gabo was a sculptor, Pevsner a painter. It was Gabo who did almost all of the work for the ballet. The curtains were made of shiny black 'American cloth', and the floor of the stage was also covered in this substance. The Constructivist sets were carried out in a form of talc known as Celon, transparent and dazzling when lit. During the funeral procession the hero's friends carried geometrical objects of wood, painted black and white. The men were given yellow tops and grey shorts, with mica accessories. Lifar had a mica breastplate, Spessivtseva a mica cone over her tutu. The only concessions to 'realism' were a toy cat and a clockwork mouse, which, like all clockwork mice,

ABOVE: *Study for the cat's costume in* La Chatte, *by Naum Gabo, 1927*

LEFT: *Serge Lifar and Alice Nikitina in* La Chatte

had a mind of its own and was eventually discarded on the grounds that it was 'inartistic'.

Some observers found all this slightly risible. Basil Maine wrote as follows, a few years later:
'Sauguet's music . . . was designed as a divan on which at any moment the ballet could lie until the next idea arrived. I recall the setting – circles, segments, ellipses and rectangles in mysterious arrangements. . . . The end, too, I well remember for its outstanding solemnity: the Young Man dies – a rigidly horizontal death – and over his body his friends perform certain rites, involving a complete set of geometrical instruments, as who should say: "We will bury him with the things he loved best".'

Here is Constant Lambert:
'The stage was cluttered up with a number of objects which, apart from looking as if they might conceivably separate milk from cream, merely served to hinder the movements of the dancers. They were, in fact, obstructionist rather than constructionist . . .'

These sour if amusing comments should not lead one to conclude that the ballet was a failure: it was a huge success. Through his choreography, Balan-

Classicism, Neoclassicism and Experiment

LEFT: *Serge Lifar and Alice Nikitina in* La Chatte. **ABOVE:** *Serge Lifar and the male dancers*

chine turned Spessivtseva into a new dancer (Diaghilev, as has been mentioned, symbolically changed her name to Spessiva) and made Lifar a star by exploiting his physical appearance while disguising his technical limitations. For the remaining life of the *Ballet Russes* Lifar was the undisputed principal attraction of the company, though still, of course, under the control of Diaghilev and his choreographers. It was only later, in the 1930s, that he got completely out of hand. The first performance of *La Chatte* was at Monte Carlo on 30 April, 1927.

The triumph was repeated at the opening of the Paris season at the Théâtre Sarah-Bernhardt on 27 May, though Nikitina had to take over the female lead from Spessiva, who had a foot injury. Stravinsky's 'birthday present' for the 20th Paris season of the *Ballet Russes* was the opera-oratorio *Oedipus Rex*, an awkward masterpiece with a good deal of spoken narration by Cocteau (who wished to deliver it himself) and a text in dog-Latin. This virtually

BELOW: *Model for the decor of* Le Pas d'acier *by Georgi Yakulov, c1927*

RIGHT: *Serge Lifar and Lubov Tchernicheva in* Le Pas d'acier

unstageable piece came as a severe shock to Diaghilev, but he gave it a concert performance between two ballets on 30 May, thus pleasing neither the composer nor the public. Neither did the audience much take to the Satie ballet *Mercure*, with choreography by Massine, which Diaghilev presented two days later. This had originally been given during Beaumont's *Soirées de Paris* in 1924, and was chiefly remarkable for the sets, carried out by Picasso in what Gertrude Stein referred to as his 'calligraphic period' and composed of pale canvas shapes 'written on' with iron wire.

Much more stirring stuff was produced on 7 June in the form of the new Prokofiev ballet *Le Pas d'acier* ('The Dance of Steel'). It was an evocation of life in Soviet Russia which amounted to an implied glorification of the regime and was thus not calculated to appeal to White Russians, rich and fashionable Paris audiences, and newspaper peers. The designs were by the Constructivist artist Georgi Yakulov and in the finale, which represented a modern factory, the decor came to life with whirring wheels, pounding pistons and flashing lights, while Prokofiev's raucous score grew to the noisiest possible climax. The earlier episodes represented scenes of Russian daily life, including one which appeared to be mocking impoverished aristocrats. This flirtation with Communism came strangely from Diaghilev, but during the previous years he had been approached on a number of occasions with tempting offers from Soviet Russia, and had taken them seriously. It should be remembered that the grim years of Stalinist Soviet Realism were still to come. What choreographer could succeed in such circumstances, especially as for some reason or other the dancers in the *corps de ballet* had one foot booted and the other bare? Yet Massine did what he could, with enthusiasm, and the ballet was a success, much admired by a number of good judges. There was very little in the way of hostile demonstration. The principal dancers were Dubrovska, Tchernicheva, Nikitina, Massine, Lifar and Woizikovsky.

The London season opened at the Prince's Theatre immediately after the Paris performances. *La Chatte* was again a great success. *Le Pas d'acier* was given in the presence of the Duke of Connaught, and the audience waited to see what his reaction would be. But either from genuine enjoyment, good manners, or Saxe-Coburg-Gotha incomprehension, the Royal Duke led the applause, which became an ovation. It was a successful series of performances, and Diaghilev left for Venice satisfied.

During the latter part of 1927 the *Ballets Russes* danced in Germany, Vienna and Geneva, and gave two gala performances in Paris. Stravinsky at last had a new ballet score for Diaghilev, and played it to him: this was *Apollon Musagète* ('Apollo, Leader of the Muses'), which had been commissioned by the American patroness Mrs Elizabeth Sprague Coolidge and would therefore be first performed at Washington, DC, the following year. But Stravinsky had kept the European rights for Diaghilev.

Apollon Musagète would obviously be one of the new ballets of the 1928 season. Diaghilev also wanted to please Lady Cunard and Sir Thomas Beecham by asking the latter to arrange a ballet to music by Handel. This was eventually called *Les Dieux mendiants* and given first in London, not Paris. The third new production was *Ode*.

This had been intended as a spectacle which would evoke the court of the 18th-century Empress Elizabeth of Russia, in whose honour the poet Mikhail Lomonosov had written a poem called the 'Ode to the Grandeur of Nature and to the Aurora

Classicism, Neoclassicism and Experiment

FAR LEFT: *Serge Lifar and Lubov Tchernicheva in* Le Pas d'acier

LEFT: *Léonide Massine and Alexandra Danilova in* Le Pas d'acier

Decor for Ode *by Pavel Tchelitchev*

Borealis'. The musical basis of the ballet was going to be a setting of this poem as a cantata by the young Russian composer Nicolas Nabokov. Kochno was entrusted with the scenario and Massine with the choreography.

It was not a simple idea, and it became very complicated indeed thanks to the chosen designer, Pavel Tchelitchev. Tchelitchev was one of the so-called neo-Romantic or neo-Humanist group of painters, whose first exhibition had been at the Galerie Druet in Paris in 1926. The others were Christian Bérard, Eugène Berman, Berman's brother Léonid, and Kristians Tonny. Both Bérard and Tchelitchev were to become famous stage designers, but while Bérard was prolific and practical, Tchelitchev became so difficult, expensive and demanding that, as a result, his genius was sadly under-used. He began as he was to continue, and *Ode* created endless problems which were not resolved until the very last moment.

Under Tchelitchev's influence the Empress Elizabeth and her court disappeared altogether. The ballet was to become a metaphysical statement about man and nature. Use was to be made of gauze curtains, phosphorescent costumes, rows of dolls suspended on cords, complicated lighting effects. The latter were devised by a film-maker called Pierre Charbonnier. Rehearsals grew more and more chaotic. Kochno and Nabokov give different accounts of what happened next, but Karsavina wrote as follows:

'Crises there were many in his [Diaghilev's] career of impresario, but few so magnificently dealt with as the one occurring in the year before his death. This was over the production of Ode. *Having left the ballet in the hands of its respective authors – the composer, the artists, the script-writer and the choreographer – all men of outstanding talent, Diaghilev to all appearances withdrew himself from the collaboration. The production, every separate element of which was excellent, showed lamentable signs of being pulled in several directions. There was no more co-ordination in it than there would be in an orchestra without a conductor. Five days before the performance, the production was still an inchoate mass of unconnected patterns: music, decor and dance would not fit into a whole. At this stage Diaghilev took the reins. He drove everybody hard, but worked himself the hardest. At the eleventh hour he pieced together the music, the choreography, the lighting, and even supervised the making of costumes. After days and nights of frenzied work, encouragement and bullying, the curtain rose on a successful performance.'*

Three male dancers, Ode, *1928*

Ode was first performed on the opening night of the Paris season, once again at the Théâtre Sarah-Bernhardt, on 6 June, 1928. The cast was headed by Lifar. It could never be a popular success, and, being so difficult to stage, it was unsuitable for touring purposes, but some of it, apparently, was strikingly beautiful. W. A. Propert wrote that, in a scene called 'Flowers and Mankind':

> *'intricate and lovely figures of flowers and men were projected on to the deep blue background, while in front of it Nature and the "Light Speck" (Lifar) played ball with an immense crystal sphere that glittered with all the colours of the prism'.*

THE SIGNIFICANCE OF *APOLLON*

Apollon Musagète followed on 12 June. It was, at least in appearance, as simple as *Ode* had been complicated. Stravinsky's score, with its echoes of Bach and Tchaikovsky, was for string orchestra alone. After a brief scene depicting the birth of Apollo, the ballet was for a *danseur noble*, representing the God, and three women dancers of ballerina status playing the parts of Calliope, the Muse of Lyric Poetry, Polyhymnia, the Muse of Mime, and Terpsichore, the Muse of Dancing. After their dances together Apollo leads the three Muses up the slope of a hill towards Parnassus, while a chariot descends to meet them. In the first production the drop-curtain and backcloth were by the primitive painter André Bauchant. The three women dancers were not in tutus but in white skirts, not unlike contemporary tennis dresses, by Chanel, with striped silk belts by Charvet, the fashionable designer of men's shirts and ties. On the opening night Lifar was Apollo, Nikitina – Terpsichore, Tchernicheva – Calliope, and Dubrovska – Polyhymnia. Danilova subsequently also danced Terpsichore, and there is every reason to suppose that she excelled Nikitina.

The threefold importance of *Apollon Musagète* can hardly be exaggerated: as a masterpiece in its own right, as a return to classicism, and as the beginning of one of the most important creative collaborations in the history of ballet, that of Balanchine and Stravinsky.

Despite the modesty of its proportions, it is possible to see *Apollon* as a great classic ballet reduced to its essentials, the three ballerinas doubling the role of the absent *corps de ballet* (20 years later Frederick Ashton's version of Stravinsky's *Scènes de Ballet* also gave the impression of being a distillation of what might have been a much longer work). There are variations for Apollo and the three Muses, a great adagio, an exciting coda and a solemn apotheosis. Balanchine's choreography is classical, but with inventive variants and modifications, now

suggesting Hellenistic sculpture, now the frescos of Michelangelo, and even the glass figures of Lalique – notably the moment when the God 'drives' the Muses like a team of horses. The ballet could be considered from one angle as one of the greatest products of the Art Déco movement.

Balanchine and Stravinsky did not work together again for Diaghilev. Their next collaboration was in 1937, on the ballet *The Card Game*, but thereafter, of course, came a stream of ballets, greatest among them, perhaps, *Orpheus* and *Agon*. The whole magnificent achievement was celebrated in the 1972 Stravinsky Festival in New York.

Apollon Musagète (now called simply *Apollo*) and *Le Fils prodigue* of 1929 are probably the only surviving Diaghilev ballets which can still be seen in

LEFT: *Serge Lifar, Danilova, Dubrovska and Tchernicheva in* Apollon Musagète

ABOVE: *Serge Lifar as Apollo*

Serge Lifar and Alice Nikitina in Apollon Musagète

Classicism, Neoclassicism and Experiment

Members and associates of the Ballets Russes on tour in Edinburgh 1928. Left to right: Roger Desormière, Serge Diaghilev, Serge Lifar, Boris Kochno, Alexandra Danilova, Lubov Tchernicheva and Felia Dubrovska

worthy and accurate productions and performances. Nijinska's *Les Noces* and *Les Biches* seem to have vanished. It is virtually impossible to form a balanced assessment of Fokine's or Massine's work because few of their ballets are still danced and fewer still as they should be. There is an immense disparity between what one reads of the original productions of such works as *Prince Igor*, *Les Sylphides*, *Carnaval*, *Schéhérazade*, *The Firebird*, *Le Spectre de la Rose*, *Petrushka*, *La Boutique fantasque*, and *Le Tricorne*, and what one sees now, if one is lucky enough to see any of these at all. *Le Tricorne*, perhaps, revives better than any of the others. But Balanchine possessed and earned the inestimable advantage of having in the New York City Ballet a company, very much still in existence, devoted to the preservation of his work (it is a pity that the Royal Ballet has shown less piety towards Ashton). This is why *Apollo* and *Prodigal Son* still live today.

The London season, which followed immediately had been financed by a committee of patronage headed by Lady Juliet Duff, Lady Ripon's daughter. Lord Rothermere was one of this group, but Diag-

FAR LEFT: *Study for Serge Lifar's costume in* Le Bal *by Giorgio di Chirico, c1929*

LEFT: *Alexandra Danilova in* Le Bal

hilev was finding him very difficult to deal with. Not only did Rothermere work through underlings whose manners left a great deal to be desired, but, unlike all the other patrons of the *Ballets Russes*, he attempted to influence artistic policy by pressing Diaghilev to eschew 'experimental' ballets. He also insisted on Nikitina being given too many leading roles. Nikitina was a good enough dancer and excellent in certain parts, but it was not for an outsider to dictate to Diaghilev in matters of casting.

During the weeks at His Majesty's Theatre the Handel-Beecham ballet was rehearsed and performed. It was put together so hurriedly that Grigoriev was horrified, but Balanchine could work very quickly if he had to. No one expected that it would last, and it was danced in costumes by Juan Gris originally used in *Les Tentations de la bergère* against one of the Bakst backcloths from *Daphnis and Chloë*. However, *Les Dieux Mendiants* or *The Gods go a-begging* was first given on 16 July with great success. The plot, by Kochno, concerned a shepherd who comes upon a group of aristocrats picnicking and instead of finding the ladies attractive is drawn to a pretty maid. This causes surprise and indignation, but at the end the shepherd and the maid are revealed as gods in disguise. The leading dancers in this pastoral were Danilova and Woizikovsky. In later years it was revived with different choreography – by Ninette de Valois for the Sadler's Wells Ballet and by David Lichine for the Ballets de Monte Carlo.

The company spent much of the autumn touring Britain, and the year 1928 ended with four performances at the Paris Opéra. Nijinsky was brought to one of these, in the hope that if he saw *Petrushka* with his former partner, Karsavina, he might be shocked out of his mental disorder. It was a vain hope, and it did not work. During one of the intervals the former star was led on stage and photographed with Diaghilev, Karsavina, Lifar, Benois and others.

It was this evening, 27 December, that Alexandrine Troussevitch, employed in a vaguely secretarial capacity by the *Ballets Russes*, had chosen to introduce Igor Markevitch to Diaghilev, an acquaintance of hers (Buckle puts the meeting earlier, but in his autobiography *Etre et avoir été* Markevitch is specific about the date). Diaghilev was understandably preoccupied by the presence of Nijinsky and merely remarked, looking at Markevitch, that it seemed a little early for him to emerge from the nursery. However, he made an appointment to listen to some music the 'child' had written.

Markevitch had been born at Kiev in 1912, of an old Ukrainian family. He was brought up in Switzerland and now, at 16, he was Nadia Boulanger's youngest pupil. He bore a distinct resemblance to the young Massine. Diaghilev was much taken by the third movement of a projected *Sinfonietta*, and he was very much taken with Markevitch as well. In fact he fell in love, undeterred – as ever – by the age difference. Before long the affair became physical. Diaghilev asked Markevitch to write a Piano Concerto which the composer was to play himself during the 1929 London season. Rieti was given the task of helping the inexperienced boy with the orchestration. If the Concerto pleased Diaghilev and the public, Markevitch was to compose a ballet.

Rieti was also writing one of the new ballets for the 1929 season, *Le Bal*, on a scenario by Kochno, while Prokofiev was working on the other, *Le Fils prodigue*. Anton Dolin was engaged for 1929, to the annoyance of Lifar, but Diaghilev and Kochno thought that Dolin would be a very suitable leading dancer for *Le Bal* and he was, of course, a star. Lifar, naturally, would be the Prodigal Son. Giorgio Di Chirico had already agreed to design the Rieti ballet, and Matisse was approached to see if he would undertake *Le Fils prodigue*. The answer was

LEFT: *Anton Dolin and Alexandra Danilova in* Le Bal, *1929*

BELOW: *Lydia Sokolova and Serge Lifar in* Le Bal

ABOVE: *Design for the decor of* Le Fils prodigue, *Scene I, by Georges Rouault, 1929*

RIGHT: *Serge Lifar in* Le Fils prodigue. FAR RIGHT: *Felia Dubrovska*

a very firm 'no', in a way providentially, since the sets and costumes which Georges Rouault eventually produced could not have been more suitable for the subject.

Diaghilev kept Lifar busy with the task of making new choreography for *Le Renard*, with a double cast of dancers and acrobats.

Le Bal had its first performance at Monte Carlo on 7 May, with choreography by Balanchine. Kochno had derived the idea from a story by the Russian Romantic Vladimir Sologub. Rieti's score was dedicated to Diaghilev, ironically, because the latter had insisted on so many changes. Di Chirico's front curtain represented the wall of a house, with three doors, and two huge naked male figures playing cymbals and dancing. The curtain rose to reveal a ballroom, with architectural fragments, classical ruins, rocks and trees; at the back a door opened during the action to reveal a white horse. The costumes of the dancers were also covered with architectural motifs, fragments of walls, columns and capitals. During a masked ball, a handsome young officer pursues a mysterious masked woman, who eventually removes her mask to reveal the face of a hag. It is her turn to pursue him. At the end, when leaving, she takes off a second mask and is once again beautiful. The officer falls to the ground. The principal dancers were Danilova and Dolin, while Dubrovska, Balanchine, Lifar and Woizikovsky appeared in Italian and Spanish dances. Some observers thought that Di Chirico's architectural obsessions had overwhelmed the ballet, others that they contributed strongly to its strange, rather nightmarish atmosphere. W. A. Propert wrote:

'Who could forget the white youths who stood sentinel by the great doors, or their sudden coming to life when they flung the doors open and we saw the white horse in the unearthly garden?'

The company was at the Théâtre Sarah-Bernhardt for the Paris season, and *Le Bal* was well received, as it had been at Monte Carlo. But the real triumph was *Le Fils prodigue*, Diaghilev's last ballet and one of his finest.

Once again, it had been Kochno's idea. He had remembered an episode in *Le maître de poste*, one of Pushkin's *Tales of Ivan Petrovitch Belkin*, when a traveller, waiting for a change of horses, sees on the wall of the room in which he is drinking tea a series of pictures representing the story of the Prodigal Son. The last of the pictures shows the boy returning home, dragging himself along on his knees. This provided Kochno with a striking visual image for the last scene of the ballet, which tells the Biblical story in simplified form. The Prodigal Son takes leave of his father, and with his two friends comes upon a group of sinister, bald-headed Egyptians. There is an orgy, and the Prodigal Son succumbs to the charms of the Siren. But she and her gang rob him, and he is left to drag himself home, destitute, to his forgiving father.

Markevitch writes that Diaghilev, though essentially a creator, always needed others to realize his ideas, and that this made him exigent to the point of tyranny. At all events he gave the composer Prokofiev a very difficult time with his score for *Le Fils prodigue*. On one occasion in 1929 Markevitch arrived at the Grand Hôtel in Paris, where Diaghilev was staying, to witness Prokofiev, not the most sensitive of men, leaving in tears. He had already rewritten the final scene of the ballet twice, but Diaghilev had insisted that he start all over again. Markevitch was shocked by this, and ventured to criticize. A few days later, when Prokofiev had come back with what was to be the final version, Diaghilev told Markevitch that this time it was he who had wept: 'It is the purest music he has ever written, and I think that, when you hear it, it will teach you to be more prudent in criticizing the way I behave.' It is indeed a most beautiful passage and the ballet is by far the best, musically speaking, of the three Prokofiev wrote for the *Ballet Russes*. And in his later ballets it was only in *Romeo and Juliet* that he attained such heights.

Rouault had been a problem. Like some other great easel painters who had worked for the ballet, he knew nothing of the stage, and it was with great difficulty that Diaghilev prised anything out of him at all. But the pastels and gouaches he eventually produced were admirably atmospheric, though Prince Schervashidze and Vera Sudeikina were obliged to work marvels to turn them into practical sets and costumes. Balanchine excelled himself with his choreographic inventions, notably the solo dance of the Siren and the extraordinary scene when the long table around which the men have been carousing is transformed into a boat, with the Siren as a figurehead and her long red cloak representing a sail.

The first night was on 21 May and it was a huge success. Whatever one may think of Lifar in general, there seems little doubt that in this particular role he was remarkable. In the last scene he made an extraordinary impression. The rest of the cast was also very strong – Dubrovska as the Siren, Dolin and Woizikovsky as the Prodigal's friends, Mikhail Fedorov as his father. In later years other leading dancers have scored great successes as the Prodigal, including Dolin himself, Francisco Moncion, Edward Villella, and, perhaps best of them all, Hugh Laing.

Before going on to London Diaghilev visited his Paris doctor, not before time. He had been unwell

Lifar and Dubrovska in Le Fils prodigue

RIGHT: *Serge Lifar and Mikhail Fedorov in* Le Fils prodigue

for months, with running sores all over his body and abscesses which refused to heal. The doctor diagnosed diabetes, prescribed a diet, and told him to rest. Insulin treatment was not available at the time. But Diaghilev would not rest – indeed he could not, at least for a while – and was lax about his diet. His health continued to deteriorate.

The London season was at the Royal Opera House, Covent Garden, and began on 1 July. Both new ballets were much liked, especially *Le Fils prodigue*. Karsavina appeared in *Petrushka*. Spessiva gave four performances of Act II of *Le Lac des Cygnes*. Sokolova was highly praised for her Chosen Virgin in *The Rite of Spring*. Neither *Le Renard* nor the new Markevitch Concerto was greatly popular, but in general the London audience was more enthusiastic than ever and there were the usual demonstrations of affection for the company.

The last performance by his company Diaghilev saw was a gala in honour of King Fuad of Egypt on 24 July. He was going to France the following day, but they were to stay on for two more performances and then go to Vichy by way of Ostend. It was at Vichy, on 4 August, that the Diaghilev Ballet gave its last performance.

Despite his medical condition, Diaghilev seems not to have considered for one moment the possibility of giving up. At the end of the Gala he went on stage, as he always did at the end of a season, to thank the dancers and bid them *au revoir* until they reassembled later in the year. He was able to tell them that advance bookings were particularly good.

Plans for new ballets were already reasonably well advanced. Markevitch's ballet – which in the end was never written – was to be based on Hans Andersen's story, *The Emperor's New Clothes*. It was called *L'Habit du Roi* and Markevitch intended to use speech and aleatory music. Both ideas sound ominous. Speech in ballet is almost always fatal (American readers with long memories may recall that at the climax of the Robbins-Bernstein *Facsimile* Nora Kaye was originally asked to yell the word 'Stop!', but the idea was abandoned almost at once). Aleatory music now has its devotees, but it is highly doubtful whether a ballet orchestra in 1930 would have been capable of productive improvization. However, both ideas were new. Hindemith, too, had been asked for a ballet, and it is possible that Diaghilev was even considering Strauss, which is surprising after the relative failure of *La Légende de Joseph*. It is quite clear that Diaghilev was turning away from what might be called the School of Paris in music.

The impresario intended going to Venice as usual. But first he wanted to take Markevitch on a whirlwind tour of Germany and Austria. His sores were still not healing, and once again his doctor urged rest. Since the company was performing at Vichy, why not join them there and take the cure?

But Diaghilev had no intention of doing any such thing. Premonitions were not lacking: when Markevitch left London to rejoin his mother at Vevey for a few days, Diaghilev had murmured, 'Everything is too beautiful. I am afraid.' He and Markevitch met at Basle and embarked on what was almost a royal tour. They went first to Baden-Baden for the festival of contemporary music. One of their happiest moments came when the composer Ernst Toch, a mediocrity without an inkling of knowledge about the dance, attempted to interest them in a ballet he had composed, explaining his libretto in heavily Teutonic French while playing the score through on the piano. The two Russians were soon reduced to helpless and painfully obvious mirth. (Diaghilev was possibly still smarting from the fact that when, full of hope and excitement, he had taken Hindemith to see *L'Après-midi d'un faune*, the response of the German composer, who had not so much as heard the music before, had been to blow an enormous raspberry. Though Diaghilev loved much Austro-German music, he did not always care for German musicians, however talented they might be.)

The next port of call was Munich, where the overawed Markevitch found himself lunching with the Richard Strausses. During one of the intervals of *Tristan and Isolde* at the Prinzregententheater, Diaghilev and Markevitch went out into the garden, and the older man suddenly started to cry. 'I said it to you in London: everything is too beautiful.' He had seen *Tristan* with his cousin Dima on his very first visit to Western Europe, and for the moment the power of the association was too much for him. He had loved Dima; now he loved Igor. And it is true that, with the *Pathétique* Symphony of Tchaikovsky, *Tristan* was Diaghilev's favourite music throughout his life. He sang a little of it to himself shortly before he died.

By now he needed daily visits from a nurse, to change his bandages. But he pushed on indefatigably to Salzburg, where he took Markevitch to hear Franz Schalk conduct *Don Giovanni*. They parted at Innsbruck station, Markevitch to return to Vevey, Diaghilev to go on, an hour later, to Venice. Again the older man wept, and blessed Markevitch as his train drew out.

Diaghilev arrived at the Grand Hotel des Bains de Mer on the Lido on 8 August. Lifar joined him at once. It did not take long for Diaghilev to realize that he was dying. On 15 August he sent for Kochno. He also sent for Misia, who, with Chanel, was cruising in the *Flying Cloud*, the huge yacht of 'Bendor', the Duke of Westminster, off the Dalmation coast. When Misia and Coco arrived they were horrified at what they saw. In the sweltering heat of a Venetian August Diaghilev was wearing his dinner-jacket in bed to try to stop himself shivering. His deterioration was rapid and he died around dawn on Sunday, 19 August.

Some of the scenes that followed were not edifying. Kochno and Lifar were exhausted and they had been obliged to suppress their loathing for each other for years. Diaghilev was scarcely cold before they went for each other physically and had to be hauled apart. There were more unseemly incidents at the burial in the Russian cemetery on the island of San Michele. As so often in such circumstances, the women took over, and made the necessary arrangements, religious, administrative and financial. It was the least, and the last, they could do for their great and unique friend.

Serge Diaghilev's death mask, 1929

Classicism, Neoclassicism and Experiment

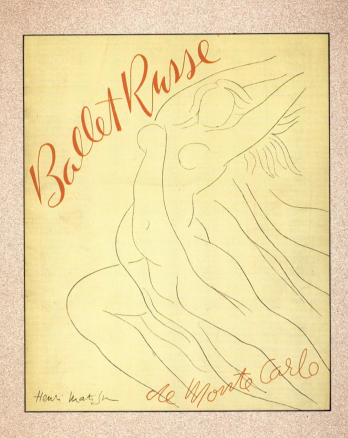

CHAPTER FIVE

After Diaghilev

DIAGHILEV WAS A unique phenomenon, and so was the Diaghilev Ballet. There has been no one quite like him and nothing quite like it since, and it is useless to pretend otherwise. When he died, various attempts were made to keep the enterprise going, but they all foundered, since there was no one available in possession of all those qualities of his which were listed in the Foreword – drive, determination, charm, resourcefulness, taste and ruthlessness – to which must now be added 20 years of running a touring ballet company through thick and thin, undertaking every task from the selection of collaborating artists to the raising, somehow or other, of money.

If Diaghilev had regarded anyone as his successor, it was Kochno, but he was not of the delegating kind. For a moment Kochno and Lifar thought they could keep things going, but they lacked the experience, the standing, the weight, and the resources, and they were both too young. In addition they loathed each other, as we have seen. And so the company never reassembled, the costumes and decors were dispersed or sold, and the dancers started looking for work elsewhere. For a time it was believed that the whole idea of the *Ballets Russes* was as dead as its creator.

Lifar was quick to see what he had to do. He had been invited to choreograph a Beethoven ballet for the Paris Opéra, and when Jacques Rouché, the Director, invited him to become *premier danseur* and permanent choreographer, he jumped at the offer. Balanchine, who might have been preferred, since while not a star dancer he was an experienced choreographer, was ill at the time and thus missed an opportunity he might have been very tempted to accept. Paris's loss was America's gain. Lifar dug himself in at the Opéra and remained there for more than 25 years, apart from a short period after the Liberation, when he was accused of collaboration. Though an unlikeable person, immensely vain, a limited dancer and a still more limited choreographer, he had the great merit of building the Opéra company up technically to the point where it was ready to be used by other, greater artists (the first of them Balanchine, in 1947). Indeed Lifar's work laid the foundations of the greatness of the company as it exists today. But it is useless to speak of the Diaghilev aesthetic in connection with Lifar.

Meanwhile, in Britain, Ninette de Valois with the Vic-Wells Ballet and Marie Rambert with the Ballet Club were sowing the seeds of the companies that were to become the Sadler's Wells (later Royal) Ballet and the Ballet Rambert. Both had absorbed Diaghilev's principles while working for him. And the Camargo Society, using Diaghilev stars like Lopokova, Markova, Spessiva and Dolin, supported by dancers from the two fledgling companies, created several good ballets. A highly talented choreographer appeared in the person of Frederick Ashton. Ironically, perhaps, in the area of promoting close and fruitful collaboration between choreographers, composers and designers, the greatest expertise was shown by Diaghilev's old enemy, Constant Lambert.

By 1931 Diaghilev's artists were scattered. The dancers had found employment where they could. Fokine was in Paris, Massine in Italy, Balanchine in Copenhagen, Nijinska in Vienna. But things were stirring in Monte Carlo.

When Diaghilev died he had left an unexpired contract with the theatre there, and the Director of the Opéra, Raoul Gunsbourg, was one of those who had hoped to carry the company on. René Blum, his highly cultivated director of ballet, devised a programme of visiting companies for the spring season of 1931, and among these was the so-called

LEFT: *Tamara Karsavina at the opening of the Diaghilev Memorial Exhibition in Edinburgh, 1954*

ABOVE: *Colonel W. de Basil*

ABOVE: *Irina Baronova and Leon Woizikovsky in* Jeux d'Enfants, *1932*

Programme cover for The Ballet Russe de Monte Carlo *by Henri Matisse*

Ballet de l'Opéra Russe de Paris, a company based at the Théâtre des Champs-Elysées and run by a former Cossack officer called Colonel de Basil. Blum and de Basil took to each other – at first – and began to work together on the idea of creating a new *Ballets Russes* to carry on the tradition of Diaghilev. Gunsbourg too was most enthusiastic.

Contracts were signed with Balanchine as *maître de ballet*, Kochno as artistic adviser, and Grigoriev as *régisseur général*. The company was to be headed by certain former Diaghilev dancers – among them Tchernicheva and Woizikovsky – and the three 'baby ballerinas', Toumanova, Baronova and Riabouchinska, for whom Balanchine and Massine were soon to create unforgettable roles.

Neither de Basil nor Blum was a new Diaghilev – de Basil's taste was not so much shaky as nonexistent, though he had a flair for cheap publicity and his talent for intrigue was unbounded, while Blum lacked ruthlessness and was altogether too kind and gentlemanly a man to be running a ballet company – but a brilliant start was made in January 1932 with the creation of *Cotillon*, a ballet devised by Kochno to Chabrier's music with choreography by Balanchine and sets and costumes by Christian Bérard. This was followed in swift succession by *La Concurrence*, with music by Auric and designs by Derain, the choreography again by Balanchine, and *Jeux d'enfants*, choreographed by Massine to Bizet's suite, with remarkable designs by Joan Miró. These ballets were up to Diaghilev's highest standards, but – apart from *Concurrence* – quite unlike anything his company had created.

However, at this point Balanchine's contract was not renewed, and he was replaced as *maître de ballet* by Massine, who was not only a highly talented choreographer but a star dancer; he also owned the costumes and notated records of much of the Diaghilev repertoire. Furthermore, his aesthetic ideas were closer to de Basil's – in as much as the Colonel had any – than Balanchine's had been.

The rest of the company's life is well-known. A four-week season at the Alhambra Theatre in London turned into a four-month engagement, and in December 1933 Sol Hurok brought them to New York for the first of their many triumphs. Later, when the company split into two (the *Original Ballet Russe* and the *Ballet Russe de Monte Carlo*), the latter settled permanently in the United States. When the rival company, Ballet Theater of New York (later American National Ballet Theater) was founded in 1940, the aesthetic ideals of the founders were essentially Diaghilevian.

This was one route whereby the ideas of the *Ballets Russes* came to the United States. However, there was another.

When Balanchine left Monte Carlo he became involved in a new project. This was *Les Ballets 1933*, a company financed by the rich Anglo-American Edward James. The company did not last long, for its existence, like that of the *Ballets Suédois* and the *Soirées de Paris*, was due to the whim of a rich amateur. But in the course of its brief Paris and London seasons it gave the first performances of no fewer than six ballets by Balanchine, to scores by, among others, Milhaud, Sauguet and Kurt Weill, and with notable sets by Bérard and Tchelitchev. Kochno was associated with this project, and in some ways it was the nearest thing to the Diaghilev Ballet to be seen after 1929 (apart

ABOVE: *Alicia Markova and Léonide Massine rehearsing Scene II of* Petrushka *for the London Festival Ballet in 1950*

FAR LEFT: *The tradition of the Imperial Russian Ballet was kept alive by Georges Balanchine in the United States, and was restated in this British production of* Ballet Imperial *which he mounted at Covent Garden with Margot Fonteyn and the Sadler's Wells Ballet in 1950*

from the *Ballets des Champs-Elysées* of the late 1940s, another Kochno project).

It was on the strength of the performances by *Les Ballets 1933* that Lincoln Kirstein, already familiar with the work of the Diaghilev Ballet, decided to persuade Balanchine to come to work and live in the United States. From this beginning sprang successively the School of American Ballet, the American Ballet itself, Ballet Caravan, Ballet Society and finally the New York City Ballet. Balanchine, often thought of in the 1920s and 1930s as an eccentric, 'marginal' choreographer, proved to be the true standard-bearer of the classic dance, as is now at last clear to everyone. Hence the Russian tradition, transmitted to Western Europe through the genius of Diaghilev, is now alive and powerful in the United States of America.

ABOVE: *Léonide Massine rehearsing* Le Tricorne *for the London Festival Ballet production in 1973*

RIGHT: *London Festival Ballet production of* Petrushka *in 1983. With Nicholas Johnson as Petrushka, Lucia Truglia as the Ballerina and Nigel Burgoine as The Moor, in Scene III*

After Diaghilev

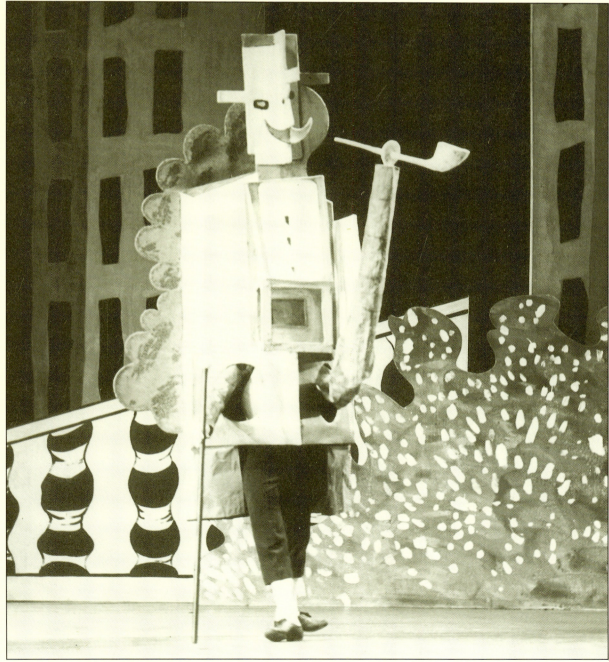

ABOVE: *The* corps de ballet *in the London Festival Ballet production of* Le Tricorne *in 1973*

LEFT: *Nigel Burgoine as the American Manager in the London Festival Ballet production of* Parade *in 1974*

ABOVE: *London Festival Ballet's production of* Parade *in 1974 with, from left: Nigel Burgoine as the American Manager, John Travis and Lorna Rogers as the Acrobats, Kerrison Cooke as the Chinese Conjuror and Carole Hill as the Little American Girl*

RIGHT: *Freya Dominic as the Persian Princess in the London Festival Ballet production of* Prince Igor *c1975*

FAR RIGHT: *Dudley van Loggenburg in the London Festival Ballet production of* Prince Igor, *c1975*

Index

Page numbers in italic refer to illustrations

A la recherche du temps perdu (Proust) 29
Academy of Arts, St Petersburg, exhibition 17
Acrobats (characters in *Parade*) 89
Acton, Harold, quoted 32
Adam and Eve (later *Romeo and Juliet*) (Lambert) 140, 142
Aesop 151
Agon (Balanchine/Stravinsky) 161
Ala and Lolli (Prokofiev) 113
Alarcón, Pedro Antonio de 90
Albany 83
Albert, Prince of Monaco 120
Albrecht (character in *Giselle*) 38
Alexander III, Tsar 38
Alfonso XIII, King of Spain 20, 83, 84, 91
Alhambra Theatre, London 94, *111*, 183
America, United States of 83, 183; see also New York
American Ballet 183
American National Ballet Theater 148
Amor bruio, El (de Falla) 90
Amoun (character in *Cléopâtre*) 23, 28
Andersen, Hans 100, 174
André (character in *La Boutique fantasque*) 95
Andrei Vladimirovitch, Grand Duke 16
Anisfeld, Boris 47
Ansermet, Ernest 83, 120, 124
Apollo (character in *Apollon Musagète*) 161, *161*
Apollo, see Apollon Musagète
Apollon Musagète (later *Apollo*) (Balanchine/Stravinsky) 119, 130, 154, 161, *163*, 167
Après-midi d'un Faune, L' (Nijinsky/Debussy) 57, *57*, *58*, 70, 83, 174
Arabian Nights 55
Aragon, Louis 142
Arensky, Anton Stepanovich 23
Armida (character in *Le Pavillon d'Armide*) 23, 24, 26, 28
Ashton, Sir Frederick 63, 130, 161, 167, 179
Astafieva, Serafine 125, 139
astrologer (character in *Le Coq d'or*) 80
Astruc, Gabriel 20, 24, 25, 30, 63, 71 quoted 22
Astuzie femminili, Le (*The Wiles of Women*) (Massine/Cimarosa) 106
Auric, Georges 116, 119, 124, 125, 132, 139, 140, 142, 183
Aurora, Princess (character in *The Sleeping Beauty*) 113, 114
Austria 29

Bach, Johann Sebastian 161
Baden-Baden 174
Bakst, Leon, 22, 29, 38, 75, 113
attends *The Sleeping Beauty* at the Maryinsky 14
costume and set designs
Après-midi d'un Faune, L' 57, 62
Boutique fantasque, La 94, *94*, *96*
Cléopâtre 30, *93*
Daphnis and Chloe 60, 63, *64*, 169
Dieu bleu, Le 48, *50*, *51*, 52, *52*, 55
Good-Humoured Ladies, The 85, *86*
Légende de Joseph, Le 77

Narcisse 43, 45, *45*
Schéhèrazade 32, *34*, 37, *37*
Sleeping Beauty, The 111, 113, 114, *114*, *116*, 119
Spectre de la Rose, La 41
Thamar 55
death 138
drawing of, by Benois *10*
engaged to work on *Sylvia* 16
portrait of Benois by *13*
relationship with Diaghilev 14, 74, 94, 120
Bal, Le (Balanchine/Rieti) 167, 169, *169*, 170–1
Balakirev, Mili Alexeivich 52, 55
Balanchine, George 101, 130, 138, 139, 140, *140*, 142, 148, 151, 154, 161, 167, 169, 170, 171, 179, 183, *185*
Baldina, Alexandra 26
Ballerina (character in *Petrushka*) 47
Ballet Caravan 183
Ballet Club (later Ballet Rambert) 179
Ballet de l'Opera Russe de Paris 183
Ballet Imperial 185
Ballet Rambert 179
Ballet Russe de Monte Carlo 183
Ballet Society 183
Ballet Theater of New York (later American National Ballet Theater) 183
Ballets 1933, Les 183
Ballets de Monte Carlo 169
Ballets des Champs-Elysées 111, 183
Ballets Russes de Monte Carlo, The (programme cover) *180*
Ballets Suédois 89, 137, 183
Barabau (Balanchine/Rieti) 140, 142
Barbier, Georges *32*, *33*
Barcelona 90
Baronova, Irina *180*, 183
Basil, Colonel W. de *179*, 183
Basle 174
Bauchant, André 161
Bax, Arnold 140
Bayadère (character in *Schéhèrazade*) *34*
Beau Gosse (character in *Le Train bleu*) 137
Beaumont, Cyril, quoted 94, 98
Beaumont, Count Etienne de 137, 154
Beecham, Joseph 48
Beecham, Sir Thomas 48, 63, 90, 125, 154, 169
Beethoven, Ludwig van 179
Benois, Alexandre 14, 22, 113, 169
attends *The Sleeping Beauty* at Maryinsky 14
costume and set designs
operas at Monte Carlo 125
Pavillon d'Armide, Le 25–6, *25*
Petrushka 46, *47*
Rossignol, Le *78*, 80, 83
drawing of Bakst by *10*
and *Le Coq d'or* 74
portrait of, by Bakst *13*
quoted 14–16
relationship with Diaghilev 14, 24, 38
Bérard, Christian 158, 183
Beriosova, Svetlana *123*, 124, *129*,*130*
Berlin 31, 52, 63, 75, 142
Berlioz, Hector 38, 125
Berman, Eugène 158
Berman, Léonid 158
Berners, Lord 145, *147*, 148, 151
Bernstein, Leonard 174
Bibiena family 114

Biches, Les (Nijinsky/Poulenc) 106, 127, *129*, 130, *130*, *131*, *132*, 132, 137, 167
Chansons dansées 128
Jeu 128
Blair, David *132*
Blanche, Jacques-Emile *38*, 45
Blue Bird (character in *The Sleeping Beauty*) 14, 26, 29, 113
Blue God (Krishna) (character in *Le Dieu bleu*) 48, *51*, 52, *52*
Blum, René 179, 183
Boîte à joujoux, La (Debussy) 70
Bolm, Adolf 26, 38, 47, 81
Bolshoi School and Ballet 10, 38, 74
Bolshoi Theatre, Moscow, 13, 14
Bonnard, Pierre *74*
Bordeaux 83, 84
Boreas (character in *Zéphire et Flore*) 139
Boris (character in *Boris Godunov*) 28
Boris Godunov (Mussorgsky) 20, 21, 70
Boston 83
Boulanger, Nadia 169
Bourman, Anatole, quoted 70
Bournonville, Auguste 13
Boutique fantasque, La 93, 94, *94*, *95*, *96*, 98, 106, 113, 167
Boyce, William 145
Brahms, Caryl 119
quoted 98, 100, 116, 140
Braque, Georges 119, 132
Breslau 75
Breton, Andre 142
Brianza, Carlotta 13–14, 113
Bride (character in *Les Noces*) 123, 124
Bridegroom (character in *Les Noces*) 123, 124
Britannia (character in *The Triumph of Neptune*) 148
British Embassy, Rome 145
Brussel, Robert 24, 62
Brussels 37
Buckle, Richard 7
quoted 22, 31–2, 55, 169
Budapest 52, 63, 83
Buenos Aires 74, 90
Bulgakov, Alexis 75, 80
Bull, John 145
Burne-Jones, Sir Edward 77
Butter Week Fair, St Petersburg 37

Cadiz 83, 90
California 84
Calliope (character in *Apollon Musagète*) 161
Calmette, Gaston 62–3
quoted 62
Camargo Society 179
Can-Can dancers (characters in *La Boutique fantasque*) 95
Carabosse (character in *The Sleeping Beauty*) 14
Card Game, The (Balanchine/Stravinsky) 161
Carmina Burana (Orff) 10
Carnaval (Fokine) 31, *32*, 38, 47, 48, 74, 93, 120, 167
Cartier (jeweller) 31
Caruso, Enrico 30
Castellane, Boni de 80
Catherine II (the Great), Empress 17
Cecchetti, Enrico 14, 47, 80, 85, 94, 101, 113, *138*
Cecchetti, Madame *138*

Century Theater, New York 83
Chabrier, Emmanuel 124, 183
Chaliapine, Feodor Ivanovich 20, 28, 70
Chanel, Gabrielle ('Coco') 20, 22, 106, 137, 161, 174
Chant du Rossignol, Le (Stravinsky) 100–1, *104*, 139, *140*
Charbonnier, Pierre 158
Charlotte, Princess of Monaco 20, 120
Charvet, fashion house 161
Chatte, La (Balanchine/Sauguet) 119, 151, *151*, *153*, 154
Chenil Galleries, London 142
Chicago 83
Chief Mandarin (character in *Le Rossignol*) 83
Chinese Conjuror (character in *Parade*) 87, 89, *89*
Chirico, Giorgio di 119, 167, 169, 170, 171
Chloe (character in *Daphnis and Chloe*) 63
Chopin, Frédéric 22, 24
Chopiniana (later *Les Sylphides*), see Sylphides, Les
Chosen Maiden (character in *The Rite of Spring*) 65, 106, *106*, 173
Chout (Slavinsky/Prokofiev) 111, 113, 120
Cimarosa, Domenico 106
Cimarosiana (Massine/Cimarosa) 106
Cincinnati 83
Cinderella (Ashton/Prokofiev) 113
Clark, Vera (Savina) 91, 94, 107
Cléopâtre (formerly *Une Nuit d'Egypte*) (Fokine/various composers) 22–3, 28–9, *28*, 30, 31, 91, 93
Cleveland 83
Cochran, C.B. 113, 142
Cocteau, Jean 31
caricature of Stravinsky 70
and *Cléopâtre* 28–9, 93
and *Le Dieu bleu* 37, 52, 87
and *Groupe des Six* 125
and *Parade* 85, 87, 89
poster of *Le Spectre de la Rose* 42
quoted 28–9, 57
relationship with Diaghilev 116
and *The Rite of Spring* 71
and *Le Train bleu* 137, *137*
and *Le Tricorne* 98
Coliseum, London 91, 138, 139, 140
Cologne 63, 75
Colombe, La (Gounod) 124
Colorado 84
Concurrence, La 183
Confidante (character in *Les Matelots*) 140
Connaught, Duke of 154
Conrad, Joseph 55
Contes russes (Massine/Liadov) 85, 93
Coolidge, Elizabeth Sprague 154
Coppélia (Saint-Léon/Delibes) 13, 94
Coq d'or, Le (Fokine/Rimsky-Korsakov) 74, 77, *78*, *78*, 89, 106, 122
Corregidor (character in *Le Tricorne*) 100
Corregidor y la molinera, El (de Falla) 90, 98
Cossack Chief (character in *La Boutique fantasque*) 94
Cotillon (Balanchine/Chabrier) 183
Cotogni, Antonio, baritone 14
Covent Garden, London 13, 48, 94, 106, *123*, 131, *132*, 173, *185*

Cuadro Flamenco 111, 113
Cunard, Lady 20, *23*, 154

Dalcroze, Jacques-Emile 63
Dancing in St Petersburg (Kchessinskaya) 16
Dandy (character in *Le Tricorne*) 100
Danilova, Alexandra
and Diaghilev 138, 142
roles
in *Apollon Musagète* 161, *161*
in *Le Bal* 167, *169*, 171
in *Les Dieux mendiants* 169
in *Jack in the Box* 142
in *Les Matelots* 140
in *Le Pas d'acier* 157
in *La Pastorale* 142
in *The Triumph of Neptune* *147*, 148, *148*
on tour in Edinburgh 165
d'Annunzio, Gabriele 70
Daphnis (character in *Daphnis and Chloe*) 63
Daphnis and Chloe (Fokine/Ravel) 29, 52, *60*, 62, 63, 169
Daudet, Lucien 29
David, see Parade
Davis, Sir Colin 125
de Valois (Devalois), Ninette 114, 125, 130, 169, 179
Death (character in *Le Chant du Rossignol*) 100
Deauville 63
Debussy, Claude 29, 37, 38, 57, *57*, 63, 70, 125
Delaunay, Robert 93
Delibes, Léo 13, 16
Delius, Frederick 140
Denmark, ballet in 13
Derain, André 93, *94*, 94, 119, 145, 183
Desormière, Roger 165
Detroit 83
Diaghilev, Sergei Pavlovitch 7, *7*, *101*
and *L'Après-midi d'un Faune* 62
Benois on 15–16
and Chanel 106
and Cocteau 87
and composers 119, 125, 145
contacts in France 29
death 174
death mask *174*
and designers 100, 113
dismisses Massine 107
dismisses Nijinsky 74
and Dolin 125–6, 138, 140
early life 7
engages dancers from Imperial Theatres, including Nijinsky 38
engages Dolin and de Valois 125
engages Kochno 111
engages Lifar 122
engages Marie Rambert 63
engages Massine 74
and England 29, 140, 142, 145, 148
European tour with Dima Filosofov 14, 174
and female patrons 20, 47, 48, 167
in financial difficulties 90–1, 116
and *The Firebird* 30–1
first London season 48
and Fokine 37, 52, 74
French contacts 29
intrigues to recruit team 16
and Kchessinskaya 16
and Lambert 142
and 'Latin' collaborators 116, 119
and Markevitch 169, 174
meets Astruc 20

188

Index

meets Picasso 83
meets Stravinsky 24
Memorial Exhibition, Edinburgh *179*
and Milhaud 137
and Misia Sert 20–1, 47
and music 106
and *Les Noces* 123–4
and *Ode* 158
and *Parade* 87
and *Le Pas d'acier* 154
personal qualities 7, 14, 91, 179
plans first season in Paris 21–5
policy as impresario 119
in poor health 171, 173, 174
and Prokofiev 171
as publisher and exhibition organiser 16, 17, 20
quoted 7
relationship with Nijinsky 23, 38, 71, 74, 83, 89–90
and *The Rite of Spring* 71
and *The Sleeping Beauty* 113–4
and Sokolova 91
and Soviet Russia 154
in Spain 83–4
and Stravinsky 37
and success of *Le Coq d'or* 78–9
on tour in Edinburgh *165*
tour of USA 83
and *The Triumph of Neptune* 148
and Vera Clark (Savina) 91, 107
visits Dalcroze school, Hellerau 63
wartime lull in career 81
Diary (Nijinsky) 23, 63, 70
Didelot, Charles-Louis 13
Dieu bleu, Le (Fokine/Hahn) 37, 38, *48*, 50, *51*, *52*, 55, 57, 87, 93
Dieux mendiants, Les (*The Gods go a-begging*) 154, 169
Dobujinsky, Mstislav 74
Dodon, King (character in *Le Coq d'or*) 74, 80
Dolin, Anton
and Camargo Society 179
joins Ballets Russes 125–6
quoted 114
relationship with Diaghilev 126, 140
roles
in *Le Bal* 169, *169*, 171
in *Les Fâcheux* 132
in *Le Train bleu* *136*, 137, *137*, 138, *138*, 140
in *Zéphire et Flore* 139, *140*
Doll (character in *Petrushka*) 48
Don Giovanni (Mozart) 174
Don Quixote (Petipa/Minkus) 74
Dresden 52, 63
Dreyfus case 30
Dubrovska, Felia
roles
in *Apollon Musagète* 161, *161*
in *Les Biches* 130
in *Les Fils prodigue* *170*, 171, *172*
in *Les Noces* 124
in *Le Pas d'acier* 154
in *La Pastorale* 142, *144*, *145*
on tour in Edinburgh *165*
Duff, Lady Juliet 20, *20*, 48, 167
Dukelsky, Vladimir 119
Dulac, Edmund 140
Duncan, Isadora 22
Durey, Louis 125

Echo (character in *Narcisse*) 45
Ecole d'Arcueil 125
Edinburgh *165*, *179*
Education manquée, Une (Chabrier) 124, 125

Edwards, Alfred 21
Efimov, Nicolai *132*, 138
Egorova, Lubov 113, 120
Elizabeth, Empress of Russia 154, 158
Emperor of China (character in *Le Chant du Rossignol*) 101
Emperor of Japan (character in *Le Chant du Rossignol*) 101
Emperor's New Clothes, The (Andersen) 174
Empire Theatre, London 100
Enchanted Lake, The (Liadov) 30
England, ballet in 13
Episodes (Balanchine/Webern) 130
Ernst, Max 119, 142
Etre et avoir été (Markevitch) 169
Eulenspiegel, Till (character in *Till Eulenspiegel*) 84

Fables (Aesop) 151
Façade (Walton) 142
Fâcheux, Les 132, *132*, 137, 140, 151
Facsimile (Robbins/Bernstein) 174
Fairy Queen (character in *The Triumph of Neptune*) 148
Faithful Betrothed (character in *Les Matelots*) 140
Falla, Manuel de 90, 98, 100
Faun (character in *L'Après-midi d'un Faune*) 57, *57*, 58
Fauré, Gabriel 84
Fedorov, Mikhail 93, 171, *172*
Felicitá (character in *The Good-Humoured Ladies*) 86
Fernandez Garcia, Felix 90, 98
Festin, Le (various composers) 26, 29, 31
Fiancée (character in *Le Dieu bleu*) 52
Figaro, Le 24, 62
Filosofov, Vladimir (Dima) 14, 174
Fils prodigue, Le (Balanchine/Prokofiev) 119, 161, 169, *170*, 171, *172*, 173
Firbank, Ronald 128
Firebird (character in *The Firebird*) 37
Firebird, The (Fokine/Stravinsky) 30, 37, *37*, 38, 47, 83, 85, 148, 167
First Bacchante (character in *Narcisse*) 43
Fitelberg, Gregor 114
Fizdale, Robert, quoted 21
Flament, Edouard 130
Flora (character in *Zéphire et Flore*) 139
Florimund, Prince (character in *The Sleeping Beauty*) 26, 113, 114
Florine, Princess (character in *The Sleeping Beauty*) 113
Flower beneath the Foot, The (Firbank) 128
Flying Cloud (yacht) 174
Fokina, Vera 31, *32*, 37
Fokine, Michel
as choreographer 94, 130, 167
works
Carnaval 31
Daphnis and Chloe 63
Narcisse 45
Papillons 74
Petrushka 47
Prince Igor 24
Sadko ('submarine' act) 47
Spectre de la Rose, Le 38
Thamar 52
as dancer
in *Carnaval* 31, *32*
in *Cléopâtre* 28
and Diaghilev 16–17, 29

quoted 31
Fonteyn, Dame Margot 63, *185*
Footnotes to the Ballet (Sokolova) 106
Four Temperaments, The (Balanchine/Hindemith) 130
Frankfurt 63
Franz (character in *Coppelia*) 13
Fuad, King of Egypt 174

Gabo, Naum 119, 151, *151*
Gaieté-Lyrique Theatre, Paris *105*, 113, 124, 139
Galerie Druet, Paris 158
Gardiner, John Eliot 125
Gautier, Théophile 38
Gayane (Khachaturian) 10
Geneva 83, 154
George V, King 41, 48, 114
Germany 29, 138, 154
Gevergeva (Geva), Tamara 138
Giselle (Coralli/Perrot/Adam) 31, 37, 38, 48, 113
Glazunov, Alexander Konstantinovitch 20, 23, 26
Glinka, Mikhail Ivanovich 10, 20, 23, 26
Goddess (character in *Dieu bleu, Le*) 52
Gold, Arthur, quoted 21
Golden Slave (character in *Schéhérazade*) 31, *32*, *35*, 83
Goldoni, Carlo 84, 85
Golliwogs (characters in *Jack in the Box*) 142
Golovine, Alexander 37
Gontcharova, Natalie 37, *38*, 74, 77, 119, *120*, 122, *122*, 148
quoted 123
Good-humoured Ladies, The (Massine/Scarlatti) 84–5, *84*, *86*, 91, 106
Goossens, Eugene 114
Gounod, Charles François 124, 151
Grand Hotel des Bains de Mer, Venice 174
Grand Hotel, Paris 171
Great Sacrifice, The (later *The Rite of Spring*) see *Rite of Spring, The*
Greffulhe, Comtesse 20
Grigoriev, Sergei 22, 74, 90, 94, 107, 120, 169, 183
quoted 85
Gris, Juan 116, 125, 126, 169
Grisi, Carlotta 48
Gross, Valentine *66*, *68*
Groupe des Six 125
Guardian of the Peace (character in *Petrushka*) 47
Guermantes, Duchesse de (character in *A la Recherche du Temps Perdu*) 20
Guidon, Prince (character in *Le Coq d'or*) 77
Gunsbourg, Raoul 179, 183
Gunsburg, Baron Dmitri de 74

Habit du Roi, L' (Markevitch) 174
Hahn, Reynaldo 29, 32, 37, 38, 52, 125
Hamburg 75
Handel, George Frederick 154, 169
Hanover 75
Haskell, Arnold 114
quoted 116
Head Eunuch (character in *Schéhérazade*) 37
Hellerau, School of Eurhythmics 63
Henriot, Emile, quoted 23
Hermitage Theatre, St Petersburg 24

Hernani (Hugo) 71
Hindemith, Paul 174
His Majesty's Theatre, London 145, 169
Hofmannsthal, Hugo von 29, 52, 63, 75, 78
Holst, Gustav 140
Honegger, Arthur 125
Hotel Continental, Paris 111
Howe, Martin, quoted 57
Hoyer 107
Hugo, Victor 71
Hurok, Sol 183

Idzikovsky, Stanislas 81, 83, 84, 85, 93, 94, 100, 101, 113, 114, 120, 142, 148
Images (Debussy) 70
Imperial Academy of Science, St Petersburg 17
Imperial Ballet, St Petersburg 14, 21–2
School 10, 13
Imperial Court, St Petersburg 13
Imperial Theatres, St Petersburg 13, 14, 16, 38
Innsbruck 174
Invitation à la Valse (Weber) 38
Iowa 84
Isvolsky 62
Italy, ballet in 13
Ivan (character in *Ivan the Terrible*) 28
Ivan, Prince (character in *The Firebird*) 37
Ivan the Terrible (formerly *The maid of Pskov*) (Rimsky-Korsakov) 26–8, 71

Jack in the Box (Balanchine/Satie/Milhaud) 142
James, Edward 183
Jeux (Debussy) 63, 70, 138
Jeux d'enfants (Massine/Bizet) *180*, 183
Jewish Dancer (character in *Cléopâtre*) 30
John, Augustus 142
Jones, Robert Edmond 84
Joseph (character in *La Légende de Joseph*) 74, 75, 77–8
Joseph in Egypt (Hofmannsthal/Strauss) 63
Joyce, James 120
Judith (Serov) 23
Jupien (character in *A la recherche du temps perdu*) 70
Juvenile and Theatrical Tinsel Warehouse, Hoxton, London 145

Kahn, Otto 83
Kansas City 83
Karalli, Vera 26
Karsavina, Tamara
at Diaghilev Memorial Exhibition *179*
and Cecchetti 14
and Diaghilev 16, 23
and Nijinsky 169
quoted 119, 158
rejoins Diaghilev 94
roles
in *La Boutique fantasque* 93
in *Carnaval* 47
in *Cléopâtre* 28
in *Le Coq d'or* 77, 80
in *Daphnis and Chloe* 63
in *Le Dieu bleu* 52
in *The Firebird* 37, *37*
in *Giselle* 37, 48
in *La Légende de Joseph* 75, 77–8
in *Narcisse* 45
in *Le Pavillon d'Armide* 23, 26
in *Petrushka* 48, 169, 173

in *Pulcinella* 101
in *Romeo and Juliet* 142
in *Schéhérazade* 32, *33*
in *The Sleeping Beauty* 26
in *Le Spectre de la Rose* 41, *41*, *42*
in *Thamar* 55
in *La Tragédie de Salome* 71
in *Le Tricorne* 100
Kastchei (character in *The Firebird*) 30, 37
Kaye, Nora 174
Kchessinskaya, Matilda, 16, 24, 38, 48, 52
Kentucky 84
Kessler, Count Harry 29, 75, 80–1
Khachaturian, Aram Ilich 10
Khamma (Debussy) 70
Khokhlova 84
Khovanshchina (Mussorgsky) 20, 70
Kikimora (Massine/Liadov) 30, 84, 85
King of Hearts (character in *La Boutique fantasque*) 93
King's Negro (character in *The Sleeping Beauty*) 113
Kirov Theatre, *see* Maryinsky Theatre
Kirstein, Lincoln 183
Kochno, Boris 111, 116, 120, 132, 142, 148, 151, 158, *165*, 169, 170, 171, 174, 179, 183
Kremnev, Nicolas 81, 91, 98, 120
Kusnetzova, Maria 75

***Lac des Cygnes, Le* (Petipa/Tchaikovsky) 14, 52, 74, 113, 173**
Laing, Hugh 171
Lalique, René 161
Lambert, Constant 125, 140, 142, 179
quoted 55, 119, 128, 142, 151
Landé, Jean-Baptiste 10
Larionov, Michel 81, 83, 84, 85, 111, 113, 119, *120*
quoted 119
Laurencin, Marie 116, 119, 127, 128, 130
Laurens, Henri 137
Lausanne 37, 81
Le Cuziat, Albert 70
Légende de Joseph, La (Fokine/Strauss) 74, *74*, 75, 75–8, 93, 174
Legnani, Pierina 13
Leipzig 63, 75
Lermontov, Mikhail 55
Levitsky, Dmitri 17
Lewis, Percy Wyndham 142
Liadov, Anatol Konstantinovich 30–1, 85
Lichine, David 169
Lifar, Serge
after Diaghilev 179
relationship with Diaghilev 122, 126, 170, 174
roles
in *Apollon Musagète* 161, *161*, *163*
in *Le Bal* 167, *169*, 171
in *La Chatte* 151, *151*, *153*
in *Le Fils Prodigue* *170*, *172*
in *Les Matelots* *121*, 140, 142
in *Le Pas d'acier* 154, *154*, *157*
in *La Pastorale* 142, *142*, *145*
in *Romeo and Juliet* 142
in *The Triumph of Neptune* *147*, 148
in *Zéphire et Flore* 139, 140
on tour in Edinburgh *165*
Likenion (character in *Daphnis and Chloe*) 64

189

Lilac Fairy (character in *The Sleeping Beauty*) 113, 114
Lisbon 90
Little American Girl (character in *La Boutique fantasque*) 94
Little American Girl (character in *Parade*) 89
Litvinne, Felia 20
Lomonosov, Mikhail 154
London
  Alhambra Theatre 94, *111*, 183
  Coliseum 91, 138, 139, 140
  Diaghilev's public in 140, 142, 151
  His Majesty's Theatre 145, 169
  La Légende de Joseph in 75, 77
  Lyceum Theatre 148
  performances at Covent Garden 48, 63, 106, 173
  Prince's Theatre 113, 154
  Royal Ballet *see separate entry*
  Royal College of Music 140
  Sadler's Wells Ballet 63, 94, 114, 169, *185*
  seasons in 38, 80, 91–3, 138, 139, 145, 148, 154, 167, 173
  The Sleeping Beauty in 114–16
  The Triumph of Neptune in 148, 151
Longues 63
Lopokova, Lydia 31, 83, 85, 89, 93, 94, 98, 113, 114, 126, 148, 179
Louis, Prince of Monaco 120
Louis XIV, King of France 126
Lvov, Prince Pavel Dmitrievitch 23
Lyceum Theatre, London 148
Lyons 63, 111

Macbeth (Shakespeare) 89
Madrid 83–4, 90, 111
  Teatro Real 84
Magician (character in *Petrushka*) 47
Mahler, Gustav 20
Maid of Pskov, The (later *Ivan the Terrible*) (Rimsky-Korsakov) 26–8, 71
Maine, Basil, quoted 151
Maître de poste, Le (Pushkin) 171
Mallarmé, Stéphane 57, 62
Managers (characters in *Parade*) 89
Maré, Rolf de 137
Marie Feodorovna, Dowager Empress 38
Markevitch, Igor 20, 169, 173, 174
  quoted 171
Markova, Alicia *138*, *140*, 179
Martinez Sierra, Gregorio 90
Martyre de Saint-Sebastien, Le (Debussy) 70
Mary, Queen 41, 48, 114
Maryinsky Theatre (later Kirov Theatre), St Petersburg 13, 14, 16, 17, 22, *24*, 38, 74, 113
  interior *10*
Massine, Léonide
  as choreographer 81, 94, 130, 142, 167
  works
    Austuzie femminili, Le 106
    Boutique fantasque, La 94
    Chant du Rossignol, Le 100
    Fâcheux, Les 132, 151
    Good-humoured Ladies, The 84–5, 94
    Jeux d'enfants 183
    Matelots, Les 139
    Meñinas, Las 84
    Mercure 154
    Ode 158
    Rite of Spring, The 106, 107
    Soleil de Nuit, Le 83
    Tricorne, Le 90, 98
  as dancer
    in *Après-midi d'un Faune, L'* 83
    in *La Boutique fantasque* 94, 98
    in *The Good-humoured Ladies* 85
    in *La Légende de Joseph* 74, 78
    in *Las Meñinas* 84
    in *Parade* 87, 89
    in *Le Tricorne* 98, 100
  relationship with Diaghilev 107, 113, 138, 151
Matelots, Les (Massine/Auric) 119, *121*, 139, *140*, *142*
Matisse, Henri 100, *104*, 116, 169–70, *180*
Mavra (Stravinsky) 119, 120
Mead, Robert *123*, *130*, *132*
Médicin malgré lui, Le (Gounod) 124
Meñinas, Las (Massine/Faure) 84
Mercure (Massine/Satie) 154
Messager, André 137
Metropolitan Opera 30
Metropolitan Opera House, New York 83
Michelangelo 161
Midas (Fokine/Steinberg) 74, 75
Milan 13
Milhaud, Darius 116, 125, *126*, 137, 183
Miller (character in *Le Tricorne*) 98, *98*, 100
Millerand, Madame 137
Miller's Wife (character in *Le Tricorne*) *98*, 100
Milwaukee 83
Minister of State (character in *The Sleeping Beauty*) 114
Minkus, Ludwig 13
Minneapolis 83
Mir Iskusstva (The World of Art) 16
  exhibition 17
Miró, Joan 119, 142, 183
Missouri 84
Molière (Jean Baptiste Poquelin) 132
Monaco 120
Moncion, Francisco 171
Monte Carlo
  audiences at 106, 125, 128, 137
  Le Bal at 170, 171
  Les Biches at 127
  La Chatte at 154
  Diaghilev bases company at 120, 122
  Diaghilev's successors at 179, 183
  Les Noces at *126*
  seasons at 52, 63, 75, 101, 119, 122, 124, 132, 139, 142, 157
  Le Spectre de la Rose at 38
Montéclair, Michel de 126
Montenegro, Roberto *41*
Monteux, Pierre 47, 70
Montevideo 74
Moor (character in *Petrushka*) 47
Mordkine, Michel 26
Moscow 10, 14, 16, 74
Munich 63, 174
Muses (characters in *Apollon Musagète*) 161
Mussorgsky, Modest 23, 26

Nabokov, Nicolas 119, 158
Naples, San Carlo Theatre 85
Narcisse (Fokine/Tcherepnine) *43*, 45, *45*, 47, 83
Natanson, Thadée 21
Nebraska 84
negro servant (character in *The Sleeping Beauty*) 116
Negroes (characters in *La Légende de Joseph*) 75
Nemtchinova, Vera 94, *98*, 101,
120, 126, 130, 140, *140*, 142
Neumeier, John 78
New York 84, 183
  Century Theater 83
  Metropolitan Opera 30, 83
  Stravinsky Festival 161
New York City Ballet 7, 148, 151, 167, 183
Newman, Ernest 100
  quoted 114
Nicholas I, Tsar 13
Nicholas II, Tsar 16, 24, 74
Nightingale, mechanical (character in *Le Chant du Rossignol*) 100, 101
Nightingale, real (character in *Le Chant du Rossignol*) 100, 101
Nights in the Gardens of Spain (de Falla) 90
Nijinska, Bronislava
  and *L'Après-midi d'un Faune* 38
  as choreographer 126, 130, 132
  works
    Biches, Les 127–8, *132*, 167
    Noces, Les 122–4, 167
    Renard, Le 120
    Romeo and Juliet 142
    Tentations de la bergère, Les 126
    Train bleu, Le *137*
  dances in *Le Train bleu* 137, *137*, *138*
  engaged by Diaghilev 113
  leaves Diaghilev 138
  pupils of 122
Nijinsky, Romola (de Pulszky) 38, 52, 62, 63, 74, 89–90
Nijinsky, Vaslav 14, *16*, 126, 169
  as choreographer
    works
      Après-midi d'un Faune, L' 38, 52, 57, 62, 70
      Rite of Spring, The 70, 71
  as dancer
    in *L'Après-midi d'un Faune* 57, *57*, *58*, 62
    in *Cléopâtre* 28
    in *Daphnis and Chloe* 63
    in *Le Dieu bleu* 37, 52, *52*, 55
    in *Le Festin* 29
    in *Giselle* 37, 38, 48
    in *Les Orientales* 38
    in *Le Pavillon d'Armide* 25–6
    in *Petrushka* 38, 45, 46, 47, 83
    in *Schéhèrazade* 31, 32, *32*
    in *Le Spectre de la Rose* 41, *41*, 45, 83
    in *Les Sylphides* 28
  dismissed by Diaghilev 74
  interned, and reconciliation with Diaghilev 83
  relationship with Diaghilev 16, 22, 23, 38, 74, 83, 90, 169
  and Romola de Pulszky 52, 74
  visits Dalcroze school, Hellerau 63
Nikitina, Alice 122, 130, 139, 142, *151*, *153*, 154, 161, *163*, 169
Noces, Les (Nijinska/Stravinsky) 10, 119, 120, 122, *122*, 123, *123*, 124, *126*, 132, 145, 167
Noverre, Jean-Georges 13
Novgorod 14
Nuit d'Egypte, Une (later *Cléopâtre*), see *Cléopâtre*
Nuits d'été (Berlioz) 38
Nutcracker, The (Ivanov/Tchaikovsky) 114
Nuvel, Walter 14, 22

Ode (Massine/Nabokov) 154, 158, 159
'Ode to the Grandeur of Nature and to the Aurora Borealis' (Lomonosov) 154, 158
Oedipus Rex (Stravinsky/Cocteau) 154
Offenbach, Jacques 137
Oiseau de feu (*pas de deux* from *The Sleeping Beauty*) 26, see also Firebird, The
Oklahoma 84
Opéra, Paris, see under Paris
Orff, Carl 10
Orientales, Les 31, 37, *38*
Original Ballet Russe 183
Orlov, Alexander 47
Orphanage, Moscow 10
Orpheus (Balanchine/Stravinsky) 161

page (character in *The Sleeping Beauty*) 119
Painter, George, quoted 29
Panaev–Diaghilev, Elena 7
Papillons (Fokine/Schumann) 74, 75
Parade (earlier *David*) (Massine/Satie) 85, 87, *87*, 94, 98, 113
Paris
  Le astuzie femminili in 106
  Les Biches in 128, 130
  Cardinal–Archbishop of 70
  Le Coq d'or in 80
  decline of ballet in 13
  Diaghilev's plans to bring Russian ballet to 20–2
  Gaieté–Lyrique Theatre *105*, 113, 124, 139
  Galerie Druet 158
  Grand Hotel 171
  Hotel Continental 111
  Opéra 20, 30, 31, 37, 75, 83, 97, 101, 119, 120, 169, 179
    Ballet 7
    rehearsals in 148
  The Rite of Spring in 70–1, 106
  Salon d'Automne, exhibition of Russian art 20
  seasons in 38, 52, 63, 113, 140, 154
  success in 29–31, 47–8
  Théâtre des Champs-Elysées 20, 63, 70, 106, 137, 183
  Théâtre du Châtelet 24, 30, 47, 52, 63, 85, 113
  Théâtre Mogador 120
  Théâtre Sarah-Bernhardt 142, 154, 161, 171
Parkinson, Georgina *131*
Pas d'acier, Le ('The Dance of Steel') (Massine/Prokofiev) 119, 154, *154*, 157
Pastorale, La (Kochno/Auric/Balanchine) 142, *142*, 144, 145
Pathétique Symphony (Tchaikovsky) 174
Pavane (Faure) 84
Pavillon d'Armide, Le (Fokine/Tcherepnine) 22–3, *23*, *24*, 25, 25–6, *26*, 48, 120
Pavlova, Anna 14, 16, *17*, 22, 23, 28, 31, 48
Pearly King and Queen (characters in *Union Jack*) 151
Péchés de ma vieillesse (Rossini) 94
Pelléas et Mélisande (Debussy) 70
Pergolesi, Giovanni Battista 100, 106
Perlouse (character in *Le Train bleu*) 137
Perm 14
Perrot, Jules 13
Peter the Great, Tsar 10
Petipa, Marius 13, 14, 113, 114
Petrushka (character in *Petrushka*)
38, 45, 46, 47, 47
Petrushka (Fokine/Stravinsky) 45, 46, 47, 47, 48, 70, 83, 167, 169, 173
Petrushka's Cry (Stravinsky) 37
Pevsner, Anton 119, 151
Philadelphia 83
Philémon et Baucis (Gounod) 124
Picasso, Pablo 83, 85, *87*, 89, 93, 98, *102*, *105*, 106, 113, 116, 119, 120, *132*, 137, 139, 154
Pierre, Prince of Monaco 20
Pilz, Maria 71
Pittsburgh 83
Poincaré, Raymond 62
Poiret, Paul 37
Polignac, Comte Pierre de 120
Polignac, Princesse Winaretta de 20, *23*, 106, 120
Pollock, Benjamin 145
Polunin, Vladimir 100
Polyhymnia (character in *Apollon Musagète*) 161
Poodles (characters in *La Boutique fantasque*) 95
Potemkin, Grigori Alexandrovitch 17
Potiphar (character in *La Légende de Joseph*) 75, 77–8
Potiphar's Wife (character in *La Légende de Joseph*) 75, 77–8
Poulenc, Francis 106, 116, 119, 125, *126*, 127, 128
  quoted 127–8, 130
Prague 63, 75
Prélude à l'Après-midi d'un Faune (Debussy) 38, 52, 57, 63
Prince (character in *Thamar*) 57
Prince Igor (Borodin) 20, 26, *26*, 38, 93, 113, 120, 167
  Polovtsian Dances 24, 26, *26*, 28, 48
Prince's Theatre, London 113, 154
Prinzregententheater, Munich 174
Prisoner of the Caucasus, The (Pushkin) 13
Prodigal Son (character in *Le Fils prodigue*) 169, 171
Prokofiev, Sergei 81, 111, 113, 119, 154, 169, 171
Propert, W.A., quoted 161, 171
Proust, Marcel 29, *30*, 32, 38, 70, 120
  quoted 29–30
Pruna, Pedro 119, *121*, 139, 140, 142, 148
Pugni, Cesare 13
Pulcinella (character in *commedia dell'arte*) 100
Pulcinella (character in *Pulcinella*) 106
Pulcinella (Massine/Pergolesi/Stravinsky) 101, *105*
Puppenfee, Die (Hassreiter/Bayer) 94
Pushkin, Alexander 13, 71, 74, 111

Queen (character in *The Sleeping Beauty*) 111
Queen (character in *Thamar*) 57
Queen of Clubs (character in *La Boutique fantasque*) 93, 94
Queen of Hearts (characer in *La Boutique fantasque*) 94
Queen of Shemakhan (character in *Le Coq d'or*) 77, 80

Rachmaninov, Sergei 20
Rambert, Marie 63, 179
Rameau, Jean Philippe 125
Ravel, Maurice 29, *31*, 63, 125
Redon, Odilon 62
Renard, Le (Nijinska/Stravinsky) 119, 120, 170, 173
René, Vicomte (character in *Le Pavillon d'Armide*) 23, 26

Respighi, Ottorino 94, 106
Revue Blanche, La 21
Revue Musicale, La 22
Riabouchinska, Tatiana 183
Ricketts, Charles 140
   quoted 45, 77–8, 80, 93
Rieti, Vittorio 116, 125, 169, 170
Rimsky-Korsakov, Nikolai Andreievitch 14, 20, 23, 26, 31, 32, 47, 55, 80, 94
Rio de Janeiro 74
Ripon, Marchioness of (formerly Lady de Grey) 20, *20*, 48, 167
Rite of Spring, The (Nijinsky/Stravinsky) 10, 37, 52, 63, *65*, *66*, *68*, 70, 70–1, 89, *106*, 106, 113, 114, 122, 173
   Adoration de la Terre section 10
   Danse sacrale 71
Robbins, Jerome 174
Rodin, Auguste 57
   quoted 62–3
Roerich, Nicolas *26*, *28*, *65*, 70
   quoted 70
Romanov, Boris 63
Rome 38, 47, 84, 111
   Teatro Costanzi 85
Romeo and Juliet (formerly *Adam and Eve*) (Lambert) 119, 140, 142
Romeo and Juliet (Lavrovsky/Prokofiev) 113, 171
Roseingrave, Thomas 145
Rosenkavalier, Der (Strauss/Hofmannsthal) 77
Rossignol, Le (Stravinsky) 74, *78*, 80, *80*, *83*, 100, *104*
Rossini, Gioacchino 94
Rosson, Keith *130*, *132*
Rothermere, Lord 140, 142, 167, 169
Rouault, Georges 119, 170, *170*, 171
Rouché Jacques 179
Rowlandson, Thomas 145
Royal Ballet, London 7, 85, *129*, *130*, *131*, *132*, 167
Royal College of Music, London 140
Rubinstein, Ida 28–9, *28*, 31, *33*
Ruslan and Ludmila (Glinka) 14, 28
   Lezginka 10, 26
Russian Embassy, Paris 62
Russian Folk Tunes (Liadov) 30
Russian Merchant (character in *La Boutique fantasque*) 94

Sadko (Fokine/Rimsky-Korsakov), 'submarine' act 47
Sadler's Wells Ballet, London, 63, 94, 114, 169, 179, *185*
St Petersburg *10*, 10, 13, 14, 16, 22, 31, 47
   Academy of Arts: exhibition 17
   Butter Week Fair 37
   Guards regiments 13
   Imperial Academy of Science 17
   Imperial Ballet 14, 21–2
      School 10, 13
   Imperial Court 13
   Imperial Theatres 13, 14, 16, 38
   Maryinsky Theatre *see separate entry*
   Tauride Palace: exhibition 17
Saint-Léon, Arthur 13
Salade (Milhaud) 137
Salle Garnier, Monte Carlo 41
Salon d'Automne, Paris 20
Salzburg 174
San Carlo Theatre, Naples 85
San Michele 174
San Sebastian 84

Satie, Erik 85, 87, *88*, 89, 98, 106, 116, 125, 142, 145, 154
Satyrs (characters in *Cléopâtre*) 30
Sauguet, Henri 119, 125, 151, 183
Savina, Vera (Clark) 91, 94, 107
Savoy Hotel, London 91, 114
Scarlatti, Domenico 84
Scènes de ballet (Ashton/Stravinsky) 161
Schalk, Franz 174
Schéhérazade (Rimsky-Korsakov) 29, 31–2, *32*, *33*, *34*, 37, 38, 48, 55, 57, 83, 93, 113, 167
Schervashidze, Prince Alexander 100, *127*, 148, 171
Schiff, Violet and Sydney 120
Schlagobers (Strauss) 78
Schmitt, Florent 63, 71, 125
Schollar, Ludmilla 120
School of American Ballet 183
Schumann, Robert 31
Scriabin, Alexander Nikolaievitch 20
Seattle 84
Selistchev Barracks, Novgorod 14
Sergei Mikhailovitch, Grand Duke 16
Sergeyev, Nicolas 113
Serov, Alexander 22, 28
Sert (Godebska), Misia 20, 20–1, 24, 29, 41, 91, *106*, 128, 174
Sert, José-Maria 21, 75, 84, 106
Seville 111
Shabelska, Maria 89
Shah (character in *Schéhérazade*) 31
Shopkeeper (character in *La Boutique fantasque*) 94
Siren (character in *Le Fils prodigue*) 171
Sitwell, Dame Edith 142
Sitwell, Sir Osbert 93, 140
Sitwell, Sir Sacheverell 93, 140, 145, *145*, 148
Sitwell family 29, 142
Slavinsky, Theodore 126, 140, *142*, 148
Sleeping Beauty, The (Petipa/Tchaikovsky) 14, *111*, 111–6, *113*, 114, *119*, 120, 126, 148
   Blue Bird *pas de deux* 26, 83, 114
   Grand *pas de deux* 114
   Grand *pas de fées* 114, 120
   Marriage de la Belle au bois dormant (Aurora's Wedding) 119, 120
   Panorama 114
   Rose Adagio 114
Sleeping Princess, The, see *Sleeping Beauty, The*
Snob (character in *La Boutique fantasque*) 94
Snowball (character in *The Triumph of Neptune*) 148
Société des Bains de Mer, Monaco 120
Société des Concerts Français 20
Socrate, Carlo 84
Soirées de Paris 137, 154, 183
Sokolova, Lydia
   joins Diaghilev 81
   quoted 91, 106–7, 126
   roles
      in *Le Bal* 169
      in *Les Biches* 130
      in *La Boutique fantasque* 94
      in *Le Chant du Rossignol* 100
      in *Las Meñinas* 84
      in *The Rite of Spring* 106–7, *106*, 173
      in *Le Train bleu* 136, 137, *137*, *138*
      in *The Triumph of Neptune* 148
Soleil de Nuit Le (Massine/

Rimsky-Korsakov) 83, 93
Sologub, Vladimir 170
Soudbinine, Seraphin 48
South America 74
Spain 83–4, 90–1, 139
Spanish Ambassador, London 113
Spectre de la Rose, Le (Fokine/Weber/Berlioz) 38, 41, *41*, *42*, 45, 47, 83, 167
Spectre de la Rose, Le (Gautier) 38
Spessivtseva (Spessiva), Olga 113, 114, 151, 154, 173, 179
Statkevitch 89
Stein, Gertrude 154
Stieglitz Museum (St Petersburg), exhibitions arranged by Diaghilev 16
Stoll, Sir Oswald 91, 113, 116, 119, 138
Stone Flower, The (Lavrovsky/Prokofiev) 113
Strauss, Richard 52, 63, 75, 77, 78, 74, 174
Stravinsky, Igor
   and Balanchine 161
   caricature of, by Cocteau *70*
   during World War I 81
   and Fokine 52
   influence on Rieti 125, 140
   meets Diaghilev 24
   and Parade 87
   relationship with Diaghilev 74, 119, 120
   and Russian folk tradition 10
   and *The Sleeping Beauty* 113–4
Stravinsky Festival, New York 161
   works
      Agon 161
      Apollon Musagète 154, 161
      Card Game, The 161
      Chant du Rossignol, Le 100
      Firebird, The 31
      Mavra 119, 120
      Noces, Les 122–3
      Petrushka 37
      Petrushka's Cry 37
      Pulcinella 100, 106
      Renard, Le 119
      Rite of Spring, The 37, 71, 107
      Rossignol, Le 80
      Scènes de Ballet 161
Stuttgart 75
Sudeikina, Vera (later Stravinsky) 111, 127, 171
Sudeikine, Sergei 71, 111
Sunday Times 114
Survage, Leopold 120
Switzerland 174
Sylphide, La (Taglioni) 13
Sylphides, Les (formerly *Chopiniana*) (Fokine/Chopin) 22, 24, 28, 93, 127, 167
Sylvia (Delibes) 13, 16
Szymanowski, Karol 114

Ta-Hor (character in *Cléopâtre*) 23, 28
Taglioni, Marie 13, 22, 48
Tailleferre, Germaine 125
Tales of Ivan Petrovitch Belkin (Pushkin) 171
Tarantella Dancers (characters in *La Boutique fantasque*) 94
Tauride Palace, St Petersburg, exhibition 17
Tchaikovsky, Pyotr Ilyich 13, 14, 26, 114, 119, 161, 174
Tchelitchev, Pavel 119, 158, *158*, 183
Tcherepnine, Nicolas 22, 23, 45
Tchernicheva, Lubov
   after Diaghilev 183
   roles
      in *Appollon Musagète* 161, *161*

in *Les Biches* 130
in *La Boutique fantasque* 93, 94
in *Les Fâcheux* 132, *132*
in *The Good-humoured Ladies* 84, 85
in *Jack in the Box* 142
in *Les Pas d'acier* 154, *154*, 157
in *Pulcinella* 101
in *Thamar* 57
in *The Triumph of Neptune* 148
   on tour in Edinburgh 165
Teatro Costanzi, Rome 85
Telegraph Boy (character in *La Pastorale*) 142
Tennessee 84
tennis champion, woman (character in *Le Train bleu*) 137
Tentations de la bergère, Les Nijinska/Montéclair) 126, 169
Terpsichore (character in *Apollon Musagète*) 161
Texas 84
Thamar (Balakirev) 52
Thamar (Fokine/Balakirev) 52, 55, *55*, 57, 93, 113
Théâtre des Champs-Elysées, Paris, see under Paris
Théâtre du Châlet, Paris, see under Paris
Théâtre Mogador, Paris 120
Théâtre Sarah-Bernhardt, Paris 142, 154, 161, 171
Theatres Annual 16
Three-cornered Hat, The, see *Tricorne, Le*
Till Eulenspiegel (Nijinsky/Strauss) 84
Times, The quoted 48
Toch, Ernst 174
Tommasini, Vincenzo 85, 106
Tonny, Kristians 158
Toscanini, Arturo 30
Toulouse-Lautrec, Henri de 94
Toumanova, Tamara 114, 183
Tragédie de Salomé, La (Romanov/Schmitt) 63, 71
Train bleu, Le (Nijinska/Milhaud) *132*, *136*, 137, *137*, *138*, 140
Trefilova, Vera 113, 114, 120, 145
Tricorne, Le (Massine/de Falla) *97*, *98*, 100, *102*, 113, 167
Tristan and Isolde (Wagner) 174
Triumph of Neptune, The (Balanchine/Berners) 119, *147*, *148*, *148*, 151
   Apotheosis 148
   Frozen Forest scene 148
Troubridge, Una 57
Troussevitch, Alexandrine 169
Tsarevna (character in *The Firebird*) 37
Tudor, Antony 130
Tug, Tom (character in *The Triumph of Neptune*) 148

Union Jack (Balanchine/Kay) 151
Utah 84
Utrillo, Maurice 119, 140

Valmouth (Firbank) 128
Vancouver 84
Vaudoyer, Jean-Louis 32, 38
Vaughan Williams, Ralph 140
Velazquez, Diego de Silva y 84
Venice 120, 174
Veronese, Paolo 75
Vestris, Auguste 13
Vevey 174
Vic-Wells Ballet (later Sadler's Wells Ballet, Royal Ballet) 179
Vichy 174

Vienna 52, 63, 154
Villella, Edward 171
Vilzak, Anatole 113, 120, 126, 130, 132
Vladimir Alexandrovitch, Grand Duke 16, 20, 24
Vladimirov, Pierre 74, 113, 114, 120
Volkonsky, Prince Sergei Mikhailovitch 16

Wagner, Richard 22, 119
Walton, Sir William 142
Warrior (character in *Le Chant du Rossignol*) 104
Washington 83, 84
Webb, H.J. 145
Weber, Carl Maria von 38
Weill, Kurt 183
Wells, H.G. 145
Westminster, Duke of ('Bendor') 174
Wicked Fairy (character in *The Sleeping Beauty*) 113
Woizikovsky, Leon
   after Diaghilev 183
   joins Diaghilev 81
   in London 93
   roles
      in *Le Bal* 171
      in *Les Biches* 130
      in *La Boutique fantasque* 94
      in *Les Dieux mendiants* 169
      in *The Good-humoured Ladies* 85, 93
      in *Jeux d'enfants* 180
      in *Las Meñinas* 84
      in *Parade* 89
      in *Les Pas d'acier* 154
      in *Les Tentations de la bergère* 126
      in *Le Train bleu* 137, *137*, *138*
      in *Le Tricorne* 100
      in *The Triumph of Neptune* 148
Wood, Christopher 142

Yakulov, Georgi 119, 154
Young Man (character in *La Chatte*) 151
Young Peasant dressed as an Old Man (character in *Petrushka*) 47
'Young Poland' group 114
Young Rajah (character in *Le Dieu bleu*) 50
Yusupov, Prince Nicholas 10

Zéphire et Flore (Massin Dukelsky) 139, *140*
Zephyr (character in *Zéphire et Flore*) 139
Zobeida (character in *Schéhérazade*) 31, *32*, *33*
Zucchi, Virginia 13
Zurich 75
Zverev, Nicolas 89, 94, 101, 130

Acknowledgments

I would like to thank my wife Pauline for her great help in matters of accuracy and style.
RICHARD SHEAD

Key: a=above; b=below; l=left; r=right; c=center

Quarto would like to thank the following for providing photographs, and for permission to reproduce copyright material. While every effort has been made to trace and acknowledge all copyright holders, we would like to apologize should any omissions have been made.

Page 6 Mary Evans Picture Library; **p.7** Hulton Picture Library; **p.8** Hulton Picture Library; **p.10** The Archives of the Royal Opera House Covent Garden; **p.11** The Fine Art Society/© DACS 1989; **p.12** The Fine Art Society; **p.15** Hulton Picture Library; **p.16** Hulton Picture Library; **p.17** Hulton Picture Library; **p.18** Sotheby's/Private Collection/© DACS 1989; **p.20/21** By Courtesy of the Trustees of the Victoria and Albert Museum/photo Baron de Meyer; **p.22** Hulton Picture Library; **p.23 a** Hulton Picture Library; **b** By Courtesy of the Trustees of the Victoria and Albert Museum/Theatre Museum, photo Hoppé; **p.24** Hulton Picture Library **p.25** Sotheby's/Private Collection/© DACS 1989; **p.26 a** Sotheby's/Private Collection/© DACS 1989; **b** By Courtesy of the Trustees of the Victoria and Albert Museum; **p.27** The Archives of the Royal Opera House Covent Garden **p.28 a** Ashmolean Museum, Oxford; **b** The Archives of the Royal Opera House Covent Garden; **p.29** By Courtesy of the Trustees of the Victoria and Albert Museum/Theatre Museum; **p.30 a** The Fine Art Society, **bl** Hulton Picture Library, **br** Sotheby's/Private Collection; **p.31** Hulton Picture Library; **p.32 al** Sotheby's/Private Collection, **ar & b** Hulton Picture Library; **p.33 a** Sotheby's/Private Collection, **b** By Courtesy of the Trustees of the Victoria and Albert Museum/Theatre Museum; **p.34** Sotheby's/Private Collection; **p.35** The Archives of the Royal Opera House Covent Garden; **p.36** The Fine Art Society; **p.37** By Courtesy of the Trustees of the Victoria and Albert Museum/Theatre Museum; **p.38** The Archives of the Royal Opera House Covent Garden/© ADAGP, Paris & DACS, London 1989; **p.39** Collection Daniel L. Katz, London © DACS 1989; **p.40** Sotheby's/Private Collection; **p.41** Hulton Picture Library; **p.42** Sotheby's/Private Collection/© DACS 1989; **p.43** By Courtesy of the Trustees of the Victoria and Albert Museum/Theatre Museum; **p.44** Bridgeman Art Library/The Fine Art Society, London; **p.45 a** Sotheby's/Private Collection/© DACS 1989, **b** The Archives of the Royal Opera House Covent Garden; **p.46** By Courtesy of the Trustees of the Victoria and Albert Museum/Theatre Museum; **p.47** Sotheby's/Private Collection/© DACS 1989; **p.48 l** Hulton Picture Library, **r** Sotheby's/Private Collection; **p.49** By Courtesy of the Trustees of the Victoria and Albert Museum/Theatre Museum; **p.50** By Courtesy of the Trustees of the Victoria and Albert Museum; **p.51** The Archives of the Royal Opera House Covent Garden; **p.52 a** Hulton Picture Library, **b** Sotheby's/Private Collection 9.6.83/46; **p.53** By Courtesy of the Trustees of the Victoria and Albert Museum/Theatre Museum; **p.54** Bridgeman Art Library/Musée des Arts Décoratifs, Paris; **p.56** Hulton Picture Library; **p.57** By Courtesy of the Trustees of the Victoria and Albert Museum/Theatre Museum; **p.58/59** The Archives of the Royal Opera House Covent Garden/photos Baron de Meyer; **p.60/61** Bridgeman Art Library/Musée des Arts Décoratifs, Paris; **p.62** By Courtesy of the Trustees of the Victoria and Albert Museum/Theatre Museum/photo Hoppé; **p.64** By Courtesy of the Trustees of the Victoria and Albert Museum/Theatre Museum; **p.65** By Courtesy of the Trustees of the Victoria and Albert Museum/Theatre Museum; **p.66/67** By Courtesy of the Trustees of the Victoria and Albert Museum/Theatre Museum/© DACS 1989; **p.68/69** By Courtesy of the Trustees of the Victoria and Albert Museum/Theatre Museum/© DACS 1989; **p.70/71** By Courtesy of the Trustees of the Victoria and Albert Museum/Theatre Museum/© DACS 1989; **p.72** Sotheby's/By courtesy of the Trustees of the Victoria and Albert Museum/Theatre Museum/© DACS 1989; **p.74** Sotheby's/From the Virginia and Ira Jackson Collection/© ADAGP, Paris & DACS, London 1989; **p.75** Sotheby's/Private Collection; **p.76** Sotheby's/Private Collection/© ADAGP. Paris & DACS, London; **p.77** By Courtesy of the Trustees of the Victoria and Albert Museum/Theatre Museum; **p.78** Bridgeman Art Library/Private Collection/© ADAGP, Paris & DACS, London 1989; **p.79** Ashmolean Museum, Oxford/© DACS 1989; **p.80/81** Ashmolean Museum, Oxford/© DACS 1989; **p.82** Ashmolean Museum, Oxford/© DACS 1989; **p.83** Ashmolean Museum, Oxford/© DACS 1989; **p.84** Hulton Picture Library; **p.85** Hulton Picture Library; **p.86** Sotheby's/Victoria and Albert Museum/Theatre Museum; **p.87** a Victoria and Albert Museum/Theatre Museum, **b** Sotheby's/Private Collection/© DACS 1989; **p.88** Hulton Picture Library; **p.89** Sotheby's/Victoria and Albert Museum/Theatre Museum/© DACS 1989; **p.90 a** Sotheby's Collection of Robert L. B. Tobin/© ADAGP, Paris & DACS, London 1989, **b** Victoria and Albert Museum/Theatre Museum; **p.91** Sotheby's/Private Collection © ADAGP, Paris & DACS, London 1989; **p.92** The Archives of the Royal Opera House Covent Garden/© DACS 1989; **p.93 a** The Archives of the Royal Opera House Covent Garden, **b** By Courtesy of the Trustees of the Victoria and Albert Museum/Theatre Museum/photo Sasha; **p.95** The Fine Art Society, London; **p.96** Sotheby's/Private Collection; **p.97** The Archives of the Royal Opera House Covent Garden/© DACS 1989; **p.98** By Courtesy of the Trustees of the Victoria and Albert Museum/Theatre Museum; **p.99** The Archives of the Royal Opera House Covent Garden; **p.100/101** The Fine Art Society, London; **p.102/103** The Archives of the Royal Opera House Covent Garden/© DACS 1989; **p.104** By Courtesy of the Trustees of the Victoria and Albert Museum/Theatre Museum/© Succession Henri Matisse/DACS 1989; **p.105** By Courtesy of the Trustees of the Victoria and Albert Museum/Theatre Museum/© DACS 1989; **p.108** By Courtesy of the Trustees of the Victoria and Albert Museum/Theatre Museum/photo Houston Rogers; **p.110** The Archives of the Royal Opera House Covent Garden; **p.111** By Courtesy of the Trustees of the Victoria and Albert Museum/Theatre Museum; **p.112** By Courtesy of the Trustees of the Victoria and Albert Museum/Theatre Museum; **p.115** By Courtesy of the Trustees of the Victoria and Albert Museum/Theatre Museum; **p.116** Bridgeman Art Library/Walter Hussey Bequest, Pallant House, Chichester; **p.117** By Courtesy of the Trustees of the Victoria and Albert Museum/Theatre Museum; **p.118** Bridgeman Art Library/Walter Hussey Bequest, Pallant House, Chichester; **p.120** By Courtesy of the Trustees of the Victoria and Albert Museum/© ADAGP, Paris & DACS, London 1989; **p.121** Sotheby's/Private Collection; **p.122** By Courtesy of the Trustees of the Victoria and Albert Museum/© ADAGP, Paris & DACS, London 1989; **p.123** By Courtesy of the Trustees of the Victoria and Albert Museum/Theatre Museum/photo Houston Rogers; **p.124/125** By Courtesy of the Trustees of the Victoria and Albert Museum/Theatre Museum/photos Houston Rogers; **p.126 a** The Archives of the Royal Opera House Covent Garden, **b** Hulton Picture Library; **p.127** The Archives of the Royal Opera House Covent Garden; **p.128/129** By Courtesy of the Trustees of the Victoria and Albert Museum/Theatre Museum/photo Houston Rogers; **p.130/131** By Courtesy of the Trustees of the Victoria and Albert Museum/Theatre Museum/photo Houston Rogers; **p.132 a** By Courtesy of the Trustees of the Victoria and Albert Museum/Theatre Museum, **b** Hulton Picture Library; **p.133** Hulton Picture Library; **p.134/135** By Courtesy of the Trustees of the Victoria and Albert Museum/Theatre Museum/© DACS 1989; **p.136** By Courtesy of the Trustees of the Victoria and Albert Museum/Theatre Museum/photo Sasha; **p.137 a** By Courtesy of the Trustees of the Victoria and Albert Museum/Theatre Museum/photo The Times, **b** Hulton Picture Library; **p.138/139 l** Hulton Picture Library, **r** By Courtesy of the Trustees of the Victoria and Albert Museum/Theatre Museum; **p.140 a** By Courtesy of the Trustees of the Victoria and Albert Museum/Theatre Museum; **p.141** Hulton Picture Library; **p.142** Hulton Picture Library; **p.143** Sotheby's/Private Collection; **p.144** Hulton Picture Library; **p.145** Hulton Picture Library; **p.146/147** Hulton Picture Library; **p.148/149** Hulton Picture Library; **p.150** Hulton Picture Library; **p.151** Sotheby's/Private Collection/By kind permission of Nina Williams née Gabo; **p.152/153** Hulton Picture Library; **p.154** By Courtesy of the Trustees of the Victoria and Albert Museum/Theatre Museum; **p.155** Hulton Picture Library; **p.156/157** Hulton Picture Library; **p.158** By Courtesy of the Trustees of the Victoria and Albert Museum/Theatre Museum/photo Lipnitzki; **p.159** By Courtesy of the Trustees of the Victoria and Albert Museum/Theatre Museum; **p.160** Hulton Picture Library; **p.161** By Courtesy of the Trustees of the Victoria and Albert Museum/Theatre Museum; **p.162/163** Hulton Picture Library; **p.164/165** By Courtesy of the Trustees of the Victoria and Albert Museum/Theatre Museum; **p.166** Sotheby's/Collection of Earle I Mack/© DACS 1989; **p.167** Hulton Picture Library; **p.168/169** Hulton Picture Library; **p.170 a** Wadsworth Atheneum, Hartford, USA/© ADAGP, Paris & DACS, London 1989, **b** Hulton Picture Library; **p.171** Hulton Picture Library; **p.172/173** Hulton Picture Library; **p.175** Sotheby's/Private Collection; **p.176** The Archives of the Royal Opera House Covent Garden/© Succession Henri Matisse/DACS 1989; **p.178** Hulton Picture Library; **p.181** The Archives of the Royal Opera House Covent Garden/© Succession Henri Matisse/DACS 1989; **p.183** English National Ballet Archives; **p.184 a** English National Ballet Archives/photo Mike Humphrey, **b** English National Ballet Archives/photo Conroy-Hargrave; **p.185** English National Ballet Archives/photos Alan Cunliffe; **p.186/187** English National Ballet Archives/photos Alan Cunliffe.